MAORI NEW ZEALAND

Discover the land
and the people of Aotearoa

ROUGH
GUIDES

Rough Guides online

www.roughguides.com

Rough Guide credits

Author: Paul Whitfield
Editor: Jules Brown
Production: Julia Bovis and Katie Stephens
Cartography: Katie Lloyd-Jones
Proofreader: Carole Mansur
Cover design: Diana Jarvis, Peter Buckley and Duncan Clark
Project Manager: Philippa Hopkins
Managing Director: Kevin Fitzgerald

Product coordination: Johnny Edmonds
Maori resource information development: Reuben Wharawhara
Rohe and Maori product information: Maori Regional Tourism
Organisations
Heritage site information: New Zealand Historic Places Trust
Joint Managing Editors: Annie Dundas and Debby Van Der Scheer

Adapted from *The Rough Guide to New Zealand* by Laura Harper, Tony
Mudd and Paul Whitfield

Joint concept by Rough Guides and Tourism New Zealand
Project managed by Remote World Ltd.

All images © DKImages

Front cover picture: © Chris McLennan
Back cover pictures: © DKImages

Printed in Italy by Legoprint S.p.A.

Introduction

Cast away in the middle of the South Pacific, some 1500km east of Australia, is the magnificent landscape of **New Zealand**. In the mythology of its indigenous people, the **Maori**, New Zealand was fished from the depths of the ocean floor by the fearless warrior, Maui. Its natural beauty, like all of creation, was the product of careful nursing by the gods, and the Maori called the land **Aotearoa** – the land of the long white cloud.

While the international success of films like the *Lord of the Rings* trilogy, *Whalerider* and *The Piano* has opened the eyes of a global audience to the stunning natural beauty that has become New Zealand's calling card, the country's **Maori heritage**, history and culture is just as vital. Traditions and practices handed down orally over the centuries are still maintained today in New Zealand, while the country's education system, politics, arts scene and social affairs are all influenced in some way by Maori culture. Even **Pakeha** (ie, non-Maori) citizens routinely use Maori words and have taken indigenous songs and dances to their hearts.

At the heart of this relationship between Maori and modern society is the **Treaty of Waitangi**, a covenant established between the Maori and New Zealand's nineteenth-century European settlers. Written in both Maori and English, and signed on February 6, 1840, the Treaty handed over governorship of New Zealand to the British and enabled peaceful land purchase for European settlement. In return the British were to guarantee and protect Maori tribal authority over their customary possessions.

Whether the British fulfilled their obligations to Maori under the Treaty is still contested to this day. Indeed, over a thousand historical claims against the New Zealand government, some dating back to 1840, are still being considered by the courts. For example, the government's attempt to sell off the state's forests in the late 1980s was thwarted by Maori, who successfully argued that while they had ceded governorship to the British in 1840, they had not given up ownership of the land and other assets. The significance of the Treaty should not be underestimated – it's very much a living document to a Maori society working diligently to re-establish its economic and cultural independence. It underpins nearly every key governmental policy decision, while issues of indigenous culture, tribal autonomy and access to education and health are inextricably linked in modern New Zealand.

The country has also adopted other Maori values evident to any first-time visitor, namely the hospitality and generosity of its people and a good, old-fashioned, can-do attitude. These traits infuse the burgeoning **Maori tourism** market, which has opened up previously neglected or under-visited parts of the country to international travellers. Whether it's the enchantment of gliding along the Whanganui River by kayak or witnessing the sun rise on sacred Mount Hikurangi on the east coast, you'll see another side of New Zealand. Moreover, as hosts, Maori can offer a comprehensive commentary on the natural environment, as well as demonstrate its traditional use in providing food and medicine. In addition, there are scores of sites and attractions throughout Aotearoa that provide a compelling background to **Maori history** – from the famous Treaty Grounds at Waitangi to the unrivalled collections in provincial museums across the country.

A parallel historical strand emphasises the influence of Abel Tasman, Captain Cook and other early **explorers**, whose first contacts with Aotearoa spelled the end of Maori hegemony over the land. Later European missionary contact left a legacy of churches and mission houses, and touring such **colonial**

heritage sites provides the necessary counterpoint for understanding how the country developed as a nation.

New Zealand comprises two major islands – the **North Island** and the **South Island** – that stretch for 1600km, encompassing an area of 268,000 square kilometres. With just four million people, most parts of the country are thinly populated, though Auckland alone has over a million inhabitants. The land is divided by Maori into **rohe** – or traditional tribal areas – that cut across contemporary provincial boundaries. The majority of Maori live in the North Island, with the largest tribe linked to the Tai Tokerau *rohe* in Northland, though the biggest *rohe* is actually that of Te Waipounamu, covering eighty percent of the South Island. Although many Maori live in urban areas away from their traditional tribal areas, their **marae**, the place from which they derive their sense of belonging, remains an integral part of their life. With over a thousand *marae* dotted around the country, **overnight stays** are becoming a regular feature of Maori tourism, and these visits provide an opportunity to engage with Maori in an intimate environment and learn some of the traditions, legends and customs that make them a unique people. **Maori festivals**, held throughout the year, also provide an opportunity to see traditional culture come alive in a tribal context.

Fact File

- To call any **telephone number** in this guide from outside NZ, dial your international access code, then 64 followed by the area code minus its initial 0, then the number.

- All prices in this guide are given in **New Zealand dollars**. Currently NZ$1 is equivalent to £0.34, US$0.63 or A$0.84.

- **Useful websites** include: New Zealand Tourism ⊛www.newzealand.com, Department of Conservation ⊛www.doc.govt.nz, and ⊛www.maori.org.nz.

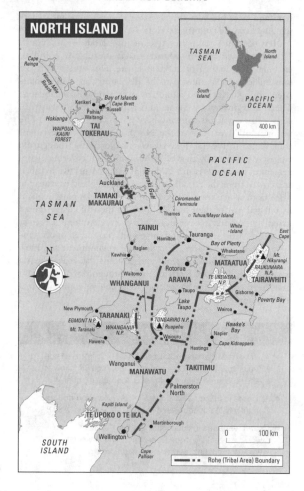

NORTH ISLAND

TASMAN SEA

North Island

South Island

PACIFIC OCEAN

0   400 km

Cape Reinga

Ninety Mile Beach

Kerikeri

Bay of Islands
Cape Brett
Russell

Paihia/Waitangi

Hokianga

WAIPOUA KAURI FOREST

TAI TOKERAU

Auckland

TAMAKI MAKAURAU

Hauraki Gulf

PACIFIC OCEAN

TASMAN SEA

Coromandel Peninsula

Thames

Tuhua/Mayor Island

TAINUI

Hamilton

Tauranga

White Island

Bay of Plenty

Whakatane

East Cape

Raglan

Kawhia

Rotorua

MATAATUA

Mt. Hikurangi

RAUKUMARA N.P.

TAIRAWHITI

Waitomo

ARAWA

TE UREWERA N.P.

WHANGANUI

Taupo

Gisborne

Poverty Bay

Lake Taupo

N

New Plymouth

TARANAKI

EGMONT N.P.

Mt. Taranaki

WHANGANUI N.P.

TONGARIRO N.P.
Ruapehu

Waiouru

Wairoa

Hawke's Bay

Napier

Cape Kidnappers

Hawera

Hastings

Wanganui

MANAWATU

TAKITIMU

Palmerston North

Kapiti Island

TE UPOKO O TE IKA

Martinborough

SOUTH ISLAND

Wellington

Cape Palliser

0   100 km

━ ━ ━ Rohe (Tribal Area) Boundary

6

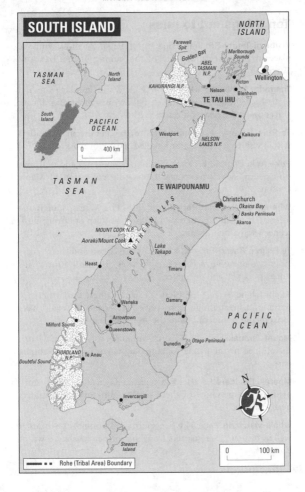

SOUTH ISLAND

NORTH ISLAND

TASMAN SEA

North Island

PACIFIC OCEAN

South Island

0 — 400 km

Farewell Spit

Golden Bay

Marlborough Sounds

ABEL TASMAN N.P.

KAHURANGI N.P.

Nelson

Picton

Wellington

Blenheim

TE TAU IHU

TASMAN SEA

Westport

NELSON LAKES N.P.

Kaikoura

Greymouth

TE WAIPOUNAMU

Christchurch

Okains Bay

Banks Peninsula

Akaroa

MOUNT COOK N.P.

Aoraki/Mount Cook ▲

Lake Tekapo

SOUTHERN ALPS

Haast

Timaru

Wanaka

Oamaru

Moeraki

Milford Sound

Arrowtown

Queenstown

PACIFIC OCEAN

FIORDLAND N.P.

Te Anau

Dunedin

Otago Peninsula

Doubtful Sound

N

Invercargill

0 — 100 km

Stewart Island

■ ■ ■ Rohe (Tribal Area) Boundary

Ten things not to miss

Waitangi Treaty Grounds Page 26 ▶ The single most symbolic place in New Zealand – site of the signing of the Treaty of Waitangi.

Tongariro National Park Page 47 ▶ A World Heritage site and natural adventure playground that showcases three magnificent volcanoes at the heart of Maori mythology.

Te Puia Page 44 ▶ Combine Rotorua's geothermal wonders with a visit to see the region's skilled artisans at work.

Puke Ariki Page 68 ▶ Combined library, museum and information centre which presents a fascinating collection of Maori treasures.

Whanganui National Park Page 73 ▶ The Whanganui is the longest navigable river in the country, with stunning bush scenery and a rich history.

Te Poho o Rawiri Page 58 ▶ One of the largest and most accessible *whare rununga* (meeting houses) in the country, it's superbly carved and decorated.

Kapiti Island Page 81 ▶ New Zealand's finest bird sanctuary provides a great insight into how New Zealand would have looked (and sounded) before the arrival of mankind.

Mount Taranaki Page 69 ▶ Iconic mountain for Taranaki Maori, surrounded by the prime walking country of Egmont National Park.

Moeraki Boulders Page 92 ▶ A typically fascinating Maori story explains the presence of these mighty surf-splashed boulders near Oamaru.

Whale-watching Page 94 ▶ See sperm and humpback whales as well as orca at close quarters from the former whaling town of Kaikoura.

Getting there

Most international airlines either fly to New Zealand themselves or have code-share arrangements with carriers that do. The main international airport is at **Auckland**, in the north of the North Island, and there's a second international airport at **Christchurch**, midway down the South Island. Christchurch receives fewer direct flights, but many airlines have a code-share shuttle from Auckland at no extra cost. An **open-jaw ticket** (flying into one and out of the other) usually costs no more than an ordinary return and means not retracing your steps to get out of the country.

Air New Zealand (ⓦwww.airnewzealand.com) has a popular daily service to Auckland via Los Angeles, with possible stopovers throughout the South Pacific. Or you can construct routes via Southeast Asia, America or Australia with the likes of British Airways, Garuda, Malaysia Airlines (MAS), Qantas, Singapore Airlines and others. If you intend to do a lot of travelling between the North and South islands, it may also be worth looking into Air New Zealand's **domestic air passes**, which have to be bought in conjunction with your main ticket – there are different fares for different zones (so you pay only for the travel you do) and you'll need to purchase a minimum of two coupons (maximum of ten).

Round-the-World (RTW) tickets, usually valid for twelve months, are another option for seeing New Zealand. These cost more than a straight return, but the route combinations are almost infinitely variable – talk to a reputable **specialist agent**, such as STA Travel (ⓦwww.statravel.com) or Trailfinders (ⓦwww.trailfinders.com), who can help with planning an itinerary.

Otherwise, a **fly-drive package** or an **all-inclusive tour** might be the way to go, especially if your time is limited and you have a fairly clear idea of what it is you want to do. Tour options range from flexible backpacker-orientated excursions to no-expense-spared, tailor-made extravaganzas, but all tend to be pretty good value – considering what you would be spending anyway to get there and around on your own.

Getting around

New Zealand is a relatively small country and getting around is easy. Ferries and catamarans connect the North and South islands, while buses and shuttle-buses are the cheapest and easiest way to travel – the rail service on both islands is very limited. Air New Zealand's domestic air passes (see "Getting there") are useful, while backpacker buses are another option, though for setting your own timetable and really getting off the beaten track, it's best to rent (or even buy) a car.

FERRIES

Interislander (ⓦ www.interislander.co.nz) ferries ply Cook Strait between Wellington (North Island) and Picton (South Island), operating year round, though bad weather does sometimes halt services. It's a three-hour trip, and advance-purchase tickets provide significant discounts on selected sailings. Most car rental companies don't allow rentals on the ferries, but they do have a pick-up place for rentals on both sides of Cook Strait.

TRAINS

Tranz Scenic (Ⓦ www.tranzscenic.co.nz) runs one train a day between Auckland and Wellington and one between Picton and Christchurch. It also operates one of the best scenic rail journeys in the world, the **TranzAlpine** – to and from Christchurch, through Arthur's Pass, stopping in Greymouth. For the best prices on all tickets you'll need to book in advance. The limited number of advanced-purchase and day-excursion fares work out cheapest, though discounts on full adult fares are available to members of youth hostel and back-packer organisations, and to senior citizens. The **Scenic Rail Pass** ($299 for a week, $499 for a month) gives unlimited access to the rail network and includes an Interislander crossing of Cook Strait.

BUSES

Public transport buses are the cheapest form of public trans-port, and services are generally reliable and comfortable. The main operators are **InterCity** (Ⓦ www.intercitycoach .co.nz) and **Newmans** (Ⓦ www.newmanscoach.co.nz), who offer a variety of passes and excursions that will get you to all major destinations. Shuttle-bus companies fill in the gaps around the country, linking with the main operators to take you off the beaten track.

BACKPACKER BUSES

Backpacker buses combine the flexibility of independent travel with the convenience of a tour. You purchase a ticket for a fixed route, then either stick with the one bus or stay in some places longer and hop on a later bus. The ticket doesn't cover food, accommodation or activities (though the latter are often arranged and discounted). The best deals are with the **Magic Travellers Network** (Ⓦwww.magicbus.co.nz), which targets independently minded travellers. **Kiwi Experience** (Ⓦwww.kiwiexperience.com) has more of a party reputation, but its routes are very popular; and **Stray** (Ⓦwww.straytravel .co.nz) is carving out a similar niche.

DRIVING AND VEHICLE RENTAL

You'll get good **car rental** deals from the major international companies, and even cheaper rates from local firms if you shop around. Vehicle rental is seasonal, with prices highest from December to February. Road conditions are generally good, though some rental companies prohibit the use of their cars on the worst metalled roads – always check local conditions before setting off. **Campervans** are very popular with visitors, too, while if you are staying in the country for more than a couple of months, **buying a used car** can be cost-effective as reselling can recoup enough of the price to make it cheaper than using public transport or renting. Most people buy cars in Auckland and try to sell them in Christchurch.

Information and accommodation

The primary sources of objective information in New Zealand are the countrywide **i-SITE visitor information centres** found in most cities and wherever tourists congregate. They're open seven days a week, handle accommodation reservations and can book transport. Most of the businesses they recommend bear the Qualmark quality standard, indicating that they have been independently assessed. **Accommodation** additionally gets a star rating from one (Acceptable; rarely used) to five (Exceptional).

Maori culture and customs

M aori culture and customs have become an intrinsic part of the New Zealand way of life. You'll often hear of **Maoritanga**, the embodiment of Maori lifestyle and culture – it is the Maori way of doing things, embracing social structure, ethics, customs, legends, art and language. All Kiwi kids, for example, grow up learning some Maori words, while opposing rugby teams quiver in the face of the New Zealand All Blacks performing the ferocious challenge dance, the *haka*. Maori artists are renowned for their intricate designs and patterns in carving, sculpting, weaving and painting, while the *hangi* (a feast cooked in an earth oven) remains a central part of communal celebrations. However, Maori culture embraces a lot more than just these outward manifestations. Characterised by the spiritual and social values of generosity, sharing, caring and service, it's derived from an oral tradition whose customs and practices predate the arrival of Maori in New Zealand.

MIGRATION AND ANCESTRY

Modern scholarship has Maori people exploring the islands that now make up New Zealand from around 1300 AD, though some date their arrival as far back as 1000 AD. There may have been canoe journeys back and forth to other Pacific islands, but it is almost certain that contact with other Pacific peoples stopped at least five hundred years ago. Maori tradition tells of their ancestors' arrival from homelands in **Hawaiki**, most likely around the Cook Islands or Tahiti. Exploratory probes by the legendary explorer **Kupe** resulted in the discovery of New Zealand, and Kupe's wife Kuramarotini named the land Aotearoa – land of the long white cloud. This was followed in 1350 by the staggered arrival of the seven fleet canoes or **waka**, from which most Maori trace their descent.

An individual's genealogy, or **whakapapa**, is fundamental to the Maori sense of place. It is still recited on formal occasions when speakers may also identify their *maunga* (mountain), *awa* (river), *iwi* (tribe) and *tupuna* (special ancestors). Even in day-to-day contact it is not uncommon for one Maori to question another with the phrase *kei whea koe?* (where are you from?), in an attempt to flag the individual's tribal identity.

IDENTITY AND FAMILY

To Pakeha (non-Maori) New Zealanders and the rest of the world, New Zealand's native people are Maori, but in the Maori world, "Maoriness" is of secondary importance. Traditionally, people's identity is more closely linked with their **whanau** (extended family), the most fundamental and tightest division in Maori society. More than a mere family social unit, the *whanau* was (and to a large extent still is) based on kinship ties, and provides an environment within which certain responsibilities and obligations are maintained. On a wider scale, people associate themselves with their **hapu** (sub-tribe) and their **iwi** (tribe) and its associated **rohe** (tribal area), its geographical boundaries passed down through oratory. The indigenous inhabitants of each *iwi* are the **tangata whenua** (literally "the people of the land").

Contemporary family structures still centre on the **marae** (community meeting place), which are helping to promote traditional arts, crafts and culture amongst urbanised Maori. Here,

On the marae

The rituals of tribal life are conducted on the **marae**, a com-bined community, cultural and drop-in centre (and much more). Strictly, a *marae* is simply a courtyard, but the term is often applied to the whole complex, comprising the *whare runanga* (meeting house), *whare manuhiri* (house for visitors) and *whare kai* (eating house). Visitors may not enter *marae* uninvited, so unless you have Maori friends or are staying with Maori you're likely to visit only on a commercially run tour. Remember that the *marae* is sacred and due reverence must be accorded the **kawa** (protocols) governing behaviour – you will be instructed as to what is required of you. First, visitors are ritually challenged to determine friendly intent. This might involve a fearsome warrior bearing down on you with twirling *taiaha* (long club), flickering tongue and bulging eyes. The women then make the **karanga** (welcoming call), which is fol-lowed by their **powhiri** (sung welcome), which acts as a pre-lude to ceremonial touching of noses, a **hongi**. On commercial trips, the welcoming ceremony is followed by a concert com-prising songs, dances and chants, and by a **hangi** (a feast cooked in an earth oven).

the basic tenets of Maori tradition remain strong, and formal protocol still reigns for ceremonies as diverse as *tangi* (funeral wakes), *hui* (meetings) and Maori exhibition openings. Wherever they reside, Maori are still more likely than non-Maori to live in extended families, indicating the continued importance of tradi-tional living arrangements. Around twenty percent of Maori live in private dwellings with extended *whanau*, and more than half of those feature three familial generations under one roof.

ARTS AND CRAFTS

Because Maori is an oratory language, **carving** in particular became a means by which Maori could record their history and *whakapapa* (genealogy). It reached its most exalted expression in the production of **waka taua** (war canoes), formidable vessels that were the focus of community pride and endeavour. Later, the *waka taua* was superseded in importance by the **whare whakairo** (carved meeting house), which came to be seen as the tangible manifestation of the *whakapapa*, usually representing a synthesis of the ancestors: the ridge-pole is the backbone; the rafters form the ribs; the gable figure is the head; and the barge boards represent arms, often decorated with finger-like decoration.

When not using wood, Maori carvers worked in **pounamu** (greenstone, or hard nephrite jade) and in pre-European times complex trade routes developed to supply Maori throughout the land from the greenstone sources on the South Island's West Coast and in Fiordland. The *pounamu* took the place of durable metals for both practical and decorative uses: adzes and chisels were used for carving, and clubs for hand-to-hand combat, while pendants took on a ritual significance and demanded decoration. Ornamental pieces ranged from simple drop pendants worn as earrings or neck decoration, to *hei tiki*, worn as a

Tattooing

A stylistic extension of the carver's craft is exhibited in **moko**, an ornamental and ceremonial form of tattooing that largely died out with European contact. Women would have *moko* just on the lips and chin, but high-ranking men often had their faces completely covered, along with their buttocks and thighs; the greater the extent and intricacy of the *moko*, the greater the status. A symmetrical pattern of the traditional elements – crescents, spirals, fern-root and other organic forms – were gouged into the flesh with an *uhi* (chisel) and mallet, then soot rubbed into the open wound. In the last decade or so the tradition of *moko* has been revived both as an identification with traditional values and as an art form in its own right; though full-face *moko* remain rare.

breast pendant and, for women, serving as a fertility charm and talisman for easy childbirth.

Meanwhile, the **weaving and plaiting** of flax and other natural fibres had long been used to create clothing, ropes and domestic implements. Plaited flax leaves formed the basis of *kete*, handle-less baskets used for collecting shellfish and *kumara* (sweet potatoes), as well as canoe sails, sandals and patterned floor mats. Both natural and coloured fibres were used in **whatu kakahu** (cloak-weaving), the crowning achievement of Maori women's art, while more robust **para** (rain capes) were made using the water-repellent leaves of the cabbage tree. Cloaks are still an important element of formal occasions, whether on the *marae*, or elsewhere, for receiving academic or state honours.

Carving, weaving and plaiting have all seen a modern resurgence, with old forms reproduced directly, and also raided as inspiration for contemporary designs. However, while it's tempting to assume that everything on sale is New Zealand made, much of the cheaper stuff is actually produced elsewhere. Consequently, the Maori arts community promotes the **toi iho** trademark, which identifies work that not only uses Maori designs and materials but that is created by a person with a cultural understanding of what they mean. Work by individuals and groups of Maori descent is labelled "maori made", with groups of predominantly Maori descent being entitled to use the "mainly maori" logo. Stockists of *toi iho* products around the country are listed on the website Ⓦ www.toiiho.com.

MUSIC AND DANCE

Music and dance play a vital role in Maori culture, passing on values and traditions from generation to generation through song, story-telling and recitation. Best known of the many so-called posture dances is the intimidating **haka** (as performed by the All Blacks), a graphic example of indigenous culture on display. While the *haka* is commonly referred to as an act of war or defiance, it is also performed to welcome, to grieve and even to protest. At commercial Maori concerts (predominantly in Rotorua but also in Christchurch, Queenstown and elsewhere) there will always be some form of *haka*, which is almost always performed by men. Though women aren't excluded from the *haka*, they normally concentrate on **poi dances**, where balls of *raupo* (bulrush) attached to the end of strings are swung around in rhythmic movements originally designed to improve co-ordination and dexterity.

The drums of eastern Polynesia seem to have been little used in Aotearoa, and both chants and the *haka* go unaccompanied. To the traditional bone flute has been added the guitar, which now accompanies **waiata** (songs), relatively modern creations whose impact comes as much from the tone and rhythm as from the lyrics. The impassioned delivery can seem at odds with music that's often based on Victorian hymns: perhaps the most well known are *Pokarekare ana* and *Haere Ra*, both post-European contact creations. Outside the tourist concert party, Maori music has developed enormously in recent years to the

The haka

The thigh-slapping, foot-stomping, tongue-poking, eye-bulging chant *Ka mate, Ka mate, Ka ora, Ka ora* ("It is death, it is death, It is life, it is life") is from the **Te Rauparaha Haka**, designed to demonstrate the fitness and prowess of warriors. It was reputedly composed in the nineteenth century by the warrior Te Rauparaha, as he lay in the *kumara* pit of a friendly chief trying to avoid detection by his enemies. Hearing noise above and then being blinded by light, he thought his days were numbered, but as his eyes became accustomed to the light he saw the hairy legs of his host, and was so relieved he performed the *haka* on the spot. Touring rugby teams have performed the *haka* at least since the 1905 All Black tour of Britain. The performance is typically led and spurred on by a player of Maori descent.

point where there are tribal and Maori-language music stations almost exclusively playing music written and performed by Maori.

MAORI FOOD

The best place to sample traditional Maori cooking methods is at a **hangi**, where meat and vegetables are steamed for hours in an earth oven and then served to the assembled masses. First the men light a fire and place river stones in the embers. While these are heating, they dig a large pit, place the hot stones in the bottom and cover them with wet sacking. Meanwhile the women prepare lamb, pork, chicken, fish, shellfish and vegetables, wrapping the morsels in leaves, then arranging them in baskets (originally of flax but now most often of steel mesh). The baskets are lowered into the cooking pit and covered with earth so that the steam and the flavours are sealed in. A couple of hours later, the baskets are disinterred, revealing fabulously tender steam-smoked meat and vegetables with a faintly earthy flavour.

Hangi aside, Maori food hasn't really crossed over into mainstream New Zealand dining. However, there are a small number of restaurants specialising in Maori fare, and some top-end restaurants (especially those with Maori chefs) are beginning to use ingredients long cherished by Maori. More commonly, you'll see **kumara** (sweet potato) made into chips or mashed (much like normal potatoes), and you may occasionally come across *puha*, a kind of thistle. Otherwise, fish and shellfish are a big part of the diet of this sea-girt nation.

LANGUAGE

The ability to speak Maori is an intrinsic part of Maori culture. For the 50,000 native speakers and 100,000 who speak it as a second tongue, it's very much a living language and forms the basis of a huge body of magnificent songs, chants and legends, lent a poetic quality by its hypnotic and lilting rhythms. The language itself shows a remarkable versatility – Don Selwyn, a Maori film director, arranged an unconventional marriage of Maori and Elizabethan English when re-creating Shakespeare's *The Merchant of Venice* for the big screen in 2002. Meanwhile, English speakers in New Zealand involuntarily pepper their speech with Maori, including greetings like *kia ora* (hello), childhood words such as *puku* (belly), *kai* (food) and *e hoa* (friend), and cultural terms like *whanau* (extended family or a bunch of friends) and *mokopuna* (grandchildren).

Although never on the brink of extinction, a survey in 1995 revealed only seven percent of Maori youth had a medium to high level of fluency in Maori. However, initiatives such as Te Kohanga Reo (Maori-language pre-schools), Te Ataarangi (new language teaching methodology), Maori-based courses and directed educational funding have provided a base from which Maori can assert their cultural distinctiveness. There are also government agencies set up specifically to develop policies and strategies to encourage widespread use of the Maori language. Meanwhile, Maori media workers in radio, television, newspapers and magazines are active in providing a Maori viewpoint, bolstered by the arrival in 2004 of the free-to-air Maori Television channel.

A Maori glossary

NB: In Maori "wh" is pronounced like an aspirated "f", as in "off"; and words don't take an "s" to form a plural.

Aotearoa New Zealand

Awa River/valley

Haka Posture dance

Hangi Earth-oven feast

Hongi Formal greeting (pressing noses)

Iwi Tribe

Kai Food

Kainga Village

Karanga Welcoming call

Kawa Behaviour protocols

Kete Woven basket

Kumara Sweet potato

Mana Prestige/status/esteem

Manuhiri Guest/visitor

Mere Fighting club

Maoritanga Maori culture and custom

Marae Tribal meeting place

Maunga Mountain

Moko Traditional tattoos

Pa Fortified settlement

Pakeha Non-Maori

Powhiri Sung welcome

Rohe Tribal area

Taiaha Long fighting club

Tangata whenua People of the land, local/original inhabitants

Taonga Treasures, prized possessions

Tapu Sacred, forbidden or taboo

Tiki Pendant shaped like a distorted human figure

Tupuna Ancestors

Wai Water

Waiata Songs

Wairua Spirit

Waka Canoe

Whakapapa Family tree/genealogical relationship

Whanau Family

Whare kai Eating house

Whare manuhiri House for visitors

Whare runanga Meeting house

Whenua Land or country

LANGUAGE

Tai Tokerau

Tai Tokerau (Northland) is Aotearoa's northernmost *rohe*, extending from the tip of the North Island at Cape Reinga to the fringes of Auckland. The *iwi* of Tai Tokerau include Ngati Kuri, Te Aupouri, Te Rarawa, Ngai Takoto, Ngati Kahu, Ngapuhi, Ngati Wai and Ngati Whatua. The *rohe* has played a pivotal role in the settlement and development of the nation, from **Hokianga** – the landing-place of Kupe, the legendary Polynesian explorer – to **Waitangi**, where the Treaty of Waitangi (1840) was first signed between the British Crown and northern tribal chiefs. Maori culture is still very much alive in this region (32 percent of the population are Maori) – indeed, **Cape Reinga** in the far north has a special cultural and spiritual significance for all Maori, regardless of their tribal affiliation. Elsewhere, quaint white churches, grand old homesteads, tiny wooden cottages and *pa* (fortified village) sites carved into the hillsides are all poignant reminders of the nineteenth-century clash of cultures that occurred in the region. The beautiful **Bay of Islands** area in particular incorporates some of New Zealand's earliest surviving European buildings. Bibles were printed in Maori in the quaint former whaling town of **Russell**; a stone storehouse and mission station were established at **Kerikeri**, now a major fruit-growing region; and an early church marks the founding of **Paihia**, today the commercial heart of the Bay of Islands.

Its historical and cultural associations aside, Tai Tokerau also enjoys a relaxed, sunny lifestyle, bolstered by its subtropical climate and myriad islands, bays and beaches. Much of the coastline remains unspoilt, and it's a premier region for surfing, boating, game fishing, sailing and diving. For more **information** consult Ⓦwww.taitokerau.co.nz and Ⓦwww.northlandnz.com.

Cape Reinga and Ninety Mile Beach

State Hwy1, 100km north of Kaitaia. Unrestricted entry. Numerous bus tours available from Paihia, plus Harrison Cape Runner tours ($40) from Kaitaia Ⓣ09/408 1033 or 0800/227 373, Ⓦhttp://ahipara.co.nz/caperunnersee.

The most northerly finger of the North Island is the Aupouri peninsula, though it is also known as **Te Hiku o Te Ika** (the

Maui hauls up a whopper

Maori mythology is littered with half-human demigods, none more celebrated than **Maui-Tikitiki-a-Taranga**. With his reputation for mischief, Maui's brothers would often leave him behind when they went fishing, but one morning he stowed away under the seats of the canoe. Far out at sea he revealed himself, promising to improve their recent poor catch. Maui egged them on until they were well beyond the normal fishing grounds before dropping anchor. In no time at all Maui's brothers filled their canoe with fish, but they scorned Maui's hook (secretly armed with a chip of his grandmother's jawbone) and wouldn't lend him any bait, so Maui struck his own nose and smeared the hook with his blood. He soon hooked a fabulous fish that, as it broke the surface, could be seen stretching into the distance. Chanting an incantation, Maui got the fish to lie quietly on the surface where it became the North Island, known as Te ika a Maui, the fish of Maui. As Maui went off to make an offering to the gods, his brothers began to cut up the fish and eat it, hacking mountains and valleys into the surface. To fit in with the legend, the South Island is often called Te waka a Maui, the canoe of Maui, and Stewart Island is the anchor, Te punga o te waka a Maui.

CAPE REINGA AND NINETY MILE BEACH

tail of the fish), recalling the legend of Maui hauling up the North Island ("the fish") from the sea while in his canoe (the South Island). Its northernmost point is **Cape Reinga** known to Maori as **Te Rerenga Wairua**, "the leaping place of the spirits". It is believed that, after death, Maori spirits travel to Cape Reinga where – using seaweed as ropes – they slide down the hill to the 800-year-old *pohutukawa* tree at the northern-most tip of the cape. The spirits make their final leap from the tree, down the roots, and then return to Hawaiki, the Maori ancestral homeland.

The spirits reach Cape Reinga along **Ninety Mile Beach** (actually around 64 miles long), a wide band of sand running along the western side of the peninsula. Each year (early March) competitors from around the world take part in the Te Houtaewa Challenge, a series of running and walking events on Ninety Mile Beach inspired by the tale of a great Maori athlete, Te Houtaewa, the fastest runner of his day.

Kerikeri Mission Station – Kemp House

246 Kerikeri Rd, Kerikeri Basin ⓦ www.historic.org.nz. Daily: Nov–April 10am–5pm, May–Oct 10am–4pm. Admission $5, combined with The Stone Store $7.

The town of Kerikeri is intimately entwined with the area's early missionary history, particularly that of the Church Missionary Society which was charged with "Anglicising" local Maori. Sole survivor of the Musket Wars of the 1820s, the **Kerikeri Mission Station** is New Zealand's oldest standing European building (1821–22), a restrained two-storey Georgian colonial affair which has miraculously survived fire and period-ic flooding. The first occupants, missionary John Butler and family, soon moved on and by 1832 the house was in the hands of lay missionary and blacksmith James Kemp, who extended the three-up-three-down design. As **Kemp House**, it's main-tained in period fashion and even the garden has seen constant cultivation since 1820.

The Stone Store and Kororipo Pa

Kerikeri Basin Ⓦ www.historic.org.nz. Daily: Nov–April 10am–5pm,
May–Oct 10am–4pm. Admission $3.50, combined with Kerikeri
Mission Station $7.

Adjacent to Kemp House, Kerikeri's **Stone Store** (1836) was
built by an ex-convict stonemason from New South Wales, and
served as a provisions storehouse, *kauri* gum trading store,
munitions depot and finally general store until bought by the
Historic Places Trust in 1976. Extensively renovated, the
ground floor store now sells goods almost identical to those on
offer 170 years ago – the once prized Hudson Bay trading
blankets, plus copper and cast-iron pots, jute sacks, gunpowder
tea, old-fashioned sweets, and preserves made from fruit grown
in the mission garden next door. The two upper floors are
devoted to a museum stocked with archaic implements including a hand-operated flour mill from around 1820, thought to
be the oldest piece of machinery in the country.

Opposite the Old Stone Store, a path along the river leads to
the site of **Kororipo Pa**, a place where in the late 1820s
Hongi Hika, a prominent local chief, had a European-style
house built. The *pa* commands a hill on a prominent bend in
the river, a relatively secure base from which attacks were
launched on other tribes using newly acquired firearms. Signs
help interpret the dips and humps in the ground.

Te Waimate Mission House

Te AhuAhu Rd, Waimate North Ⓦ www.historic.org.nz. Daily
10am–5pm (26 Dec–30 April), May–Oct Sat & Sun only 10am–5pm,
Sat–Wed 10am–5pm (1 Nov–24 Dec). Admission $7.50.

Te Waimate Mission House is New Zealand's second-oldest
European building. Now pretty much in the middle of
nowhere, in the 1830s this was the centre of a vigorous
Anglican mission, the first to be established on an inland site
chosen for its fertile soils and large Maori population. By 1834
Maori were growing wheat which was being milled at the

THE STONE STORE AND KORORIPO PA

river, orchards were flourishing and crops were sprouting – all duly impressing Charles Darwin, who visited the following year. Though modified over the years, the house has been accurately restored and stocked with period furniture and personal effects, giving some insight into the early mission lifestyle.

Waitangi Treaty Grounds

1 Tau Henare Drive, Waitangi Ⓦ www.waitangi.net.nz. Daily: Oct–March 9am–6pm, April–Sept 9am–5pm. Admission $10, for cultural show see listings.

The **Waitangi Treaty Grounds** form the single most symbolic place in New Zealand for Maori and non-Maori alike. It was here that Queen Victoria's representative, William Hobson, and nearly fifty Maori chiefs signed the Treat of Waitangi, ceding Aotearoa's governorship to Britain, whilst ostensibly affording the Maori protection and guaranteeing them rights over land and resources.

The Treaty of Waitangi

The **Treaty of Waitangi**, the founding document of modern New Zealand, was signed in 1840 between what were ostensibly two sovereign states – the United Kingdom and the United Tribes of New Zealand – and remains central to New Zealand's race relations. Motivated in part by a desire to staunch French expansion in the Pacific, the British instructed naval captain William Hobson to negotiate the transfer of sovereignty and to deal fairly with the Maori. Hobson and others drew up both the English Treaty and a Maori translation, which was unveiled in Waitangi in front of four hundred representatives of the five northern tribes. Presented as a contract between the chiefs and Queen Victoria, the benefits were amplified and the costs downplayed. As most chiefs didn't understand English, they signed the Maori version, which still has *mana* (prestige) among Maori today.

The **Treaty House** was built in 1833–34 for British Resident (representative) James Busby who was sent to New Zealand to act as a mediator for the British. The building has been added to several times though the current display shows clearly the original four-room cottage, now "a house within a house". Prompted by the pending 150th anniversary of the Treaty signing in 1990, the house was stripped back to reveal the original simplicity of the Residency building.

The other prominent building in the historic precinct is the **whare runanga**, a carved meeting house built by Maori to commemorate the centenary of the signing of the Treaty of Waitangi. Unlike most meeting houses, which are built as a monument to a particular tribe and their ancestors, this one represents all the tribes of Aotearoa. Because Waitangi's *whare runanga* is in Ngapuhi's tribal area, pride of place has been given to carvings of Ngapuhi ancestors Hineamaru and Rahiri. Inside, however, 28 carvings from regions all over New Zealand describe each tribe's ancestral stories in styles distinctive to that region.

Pompallier

The Strand, Russell Ⓦ www.historic.org.nz. Dec–April daily 10am–5pm, May–Nov daily guided tours only at 10.15am, 11.15am, 1.15pm, 2.15pm & 3.15pm. Admission $7.50.

Russell's most striking structure is **Pompallier**, the last surviving building of what was once the most important Catholic mission in the western Pacific. Completed in 1842 of rammed earth, and incorporating a tannery and printing press, it produced Catholic texts in Maori until 1850. Long used as a house, it has now been restored to its original condition, complete with hipped roof and broad eaves, and operates as a museum. It is an austere place of wooden floors and lime-washed walls where displays chart the changes the house has undergone, and artisans are again producing handmade books. Outside, the grounds have been restored to late nineteenth-century grandeur, a perfect place for a picnic.

POMPALLIER

27

Flagstaff Hill

Off Tapeka Rd, 1km north of Russell. Unrestricted access. For dawn service information, call Lorraine Hill on ⊤ 09/403 7504.

Flagstaff Hill (Maiki), with its Bay of Islands views, is surmounted by the most famous flagpole in New Zealand. Soon after the 1840 signing of the Treaty of Waitangi, the capital (previously Russell) was moved to Auckland and the subsequent loss of trade brought the first tangible expression of dissent from Maori. Ngapuhi leader Hone Heke felled this most fundamental symbol of British authority a total of four times, the last in 1843. The current pole was erected twelve years later and has stayed put, and the old Maori Confederation of Tribes flag is still flown on significant days of the year, such as the anniversary of Hone Heke's death and the final day of the first New Zealand War. The local Maori community also holds a ceremonial dawn service on March 11 each year, marking the start of the first Maori War in 1845.

Urupukapuka Island

Access by boat from Paihia with Fullers ⊤ 09/402 7421, Ⓦ www.fullers-bay-of-islands.co.nz. Cruises from $70, overnight stays $20–30 per person.

Earthworks from *pa* sites can be found on headlands all round the Bay of Islands, but some of the more intriguing can be found on **Urupukapuka Island**, the only island in the Bay that has overnight guest accommodation. Although the island is now used for sheep farming, Maori lived here for hundreds of years, and left evidence in the form of village earthworks and *kumara* (sweet potato) pits. These can be seen on an archaeological walk (3–4hr) that loops around the coast. The land was leased for grazing in the late 1800s, and in 1927 the island's Otehei Bay became a big-game fishing base popularised by American western writer, Zane Grey.

Cape Brett

Eastern Bay of Islands. Access along the Cape Brett Track (20km each way) and with Cape Brett Walkways (see listing below).

The **Cape Brett** peninsula casts a protecting arm around the Bay of Islands, its wild ridges and wave-smashed bays a dramatic contrast to the sheltered waters within. Captain Cook named the peninsula after one of the lords of the Admiralty but to Maori it is **Rakaumangamanga Mai Hawaiki Herenga Waka o Nga Tupuna** – "branch of many tribes from our origins of Hawaiki, the gathering place of the canoes of our ancestors". Seven peaks along the main ridgeline represent the seven canoes of the Great Migration from eastern Polynesia, and the peninsula is one apex of the Polynesian triangle along with Hawaii and Easter Island. Maori own two thirds of the peninsula, but the outermost third is public land accessed by the Cape Brett Track (8hr each way from the Maori village of Rawhiti). The track finishes at a lighthouse complex where a former keeper's house is a Department of Conservation overnight hut.

Hokianga Harbour

Northland west coast, 125km west of the Bay of Islands.

South of Kaitaia, the narrow, mangrove-flanked fissures of the **Hokianga Harbour** snake deep inland past tiny communities. It was from the Hokianga that the great Polynesian explorer Kupe left Aotearoa to go back to his homeland in Hawaiki and the harbour thus became known as **Hokianganui-a-Kupe**, the place of Kupe's great return. You are likely to spend most of your time on the southern shores, from where the harbour's striking, deep-blue waters beautifully set off the mountainous sand dunes of North Head. The dunes are best seen from the rocky promontory of South Head, high above the treacherous Hokianga Bar, or reached by boat for a little sand tobogganing. The high forest ranges immediately to the south make excellent hiking and horse-trekking territory and Waipoua Forest is within striking distance.

Waipoua Forest

State Hwy 12, 20km south of the Hokianga Harbour
Ⓦ www.waipoua.org.nz. Unrestricted access.

Tai Tokerau was once covered in mixed forest dominated by the mighty **kauri**, a species of pine tree, which now grows only in New Zealand. It's the world's second-largest tree (after the Californian redwoods) with a fat, barely tapering trunk that provides huge quantities of timber. Maori used it for carving and for building boats and housing, while the gum was used for starting fires and chewing (after it had been soaked in water and mixed with the milk of the *puha* plant). A short path leads through **Waipoua Forest** to New Zealand's mightiest tree, the 1200-year-old **Tane Mahuta**. A vast wall of bark 6m wide rises up nearly 18m to the lowest branches, where it seems that half the forest's epiphytes have lodged in the crook. The tree takes its name from the God of the Forest, who plays a prominent role in the Maori creation story where Ranginui, the "Sky Father", and Papatuanuku, the "Earth Mother", clung to each other so tightly that no light could penetrate between them and their children had no room to move. Eventually they called on Tane Mahuta, who lay on Papa and shoved Rangi up into the heavens, thereby letting light into the world.

A second path finds its way to **Te Matua Ngahere**, the "Father of the Forest", ranked as the second largest tree on account of its shorter stature but, if anything, more richly festooned in epiphytes than its big brother.

MAORI CULTURAL EXPERIENCES

Cape Brett Walkways
☏ 09/403 8823, Ⓦ www
.capebrettwalks.co.nz. The
"Rakaumangamanga Freedom
Walk" (return track fee $30)
allows you simply to walk from
Rawhiti to Cape Brett (and stay
overnight at the DOC hut, $12),
though boat-supported walking
tours ($325, minimum two
people) include lunch and an
insight into local Maori culture.
Footprints Waipoua ☏ 09/405
8737, Ⓦ www.omapere.co.nz.

Four-hour guided night walks ($55) – with ecological and cultural interpretation – through New Zealand's largest *kauri* forest.

Manaia Lodge Mitimiti, Hokianga Harbour ☏ 09/409 5347, ✉ mitimiti@xtra.co.nz. Maori-run backpackers' lodge (accommodation $25 per person) in a remote coastal community, which has strong traditions associated with Nukutawhiti, grandson of Kupe. Half-day cultural tours ($30) visit the carvings at the local Matihetihe *marae*.

Pakiri Beach Horse Rides ☏ 09/422 6275, ⓦ www .horseride-nz.co.nz. Rides of all kinds at Pakiri, 80km north of Auckland, from short beach jaunts and moonlight rides (from $40) to the five-day "Warrior Trail" ($2295).

Pukematu Lodge Russell ☏ 09/403 8500, ⓦ www.pukematulodge.co.nz. Accommodation in luxurious suites (from $350), with great sea views and surrounding bush alive with birdlife. You're hosted by a Maori family with deep roots in the area and a passion for local culture.

Taharangi Marie Lodge Ninety Mile Beach ☏ 09/406 7462, ⓦ www.90mile.co.nz.

Comfortable, isolated B&B (Maori for "Peaceful Horizon") beside Ninety Mile Beach, run by people well versed in their Maori heritage.

Taiamai Tours Heritage Journeys ☏ 09/405 9990, ⓦ www.taiamaitours.co.nz. Paddle out into the Bay of Islands from Paihia in a traditional-style canoe as your Ngapuhi hosts, dressed as warriors, dive for *kai moana* (seafood) and relate local legends. Oct–April Mon–Sat at 10am, 1pm & 3pm, $50.

Te Puna i Keteriki Moerewa ⓦ www.tuna.maori.nz. This intriguing collection of Maori businesses on State Hwy 1, 20km southeast of Paihia, comes complete with café, hair salon, contemporary Maori clothing company, and art gallery.

Treaty of Waitangi Night Show ☏ 09/402 5990, ⓦ www.culturenorth.co.nz. This contemporary approach to presenting Maori culture at the Waitangi Treaty Grounds retains the dance element but uses an elder relating local history to weave it all together. Book in advance for shows. Mon, Wed, Thurs & Sat (Oct–April), other nights by arrangement; admission $45.

MAORI CULTURAL EXPERIENCES

●

Tamaki Makaurau

Auckland, New Zealand's largest and most vibrant and cosmopolitan city, occupies the *rohe* of **Tamaki Makaurau**. As home to the country's major international airport it is likely to be your introduction to Aotearoa. Tamaki Makaurau actually stretches around 100km from Puhoi, in the north, to Pokeno, south of the Bombay Hills, and takes in the Kaipara Harbour and Auckland's wild west coast, the location for the filming of *The Piano*. On the east coast, the Hauraki Gulf was the backdrop for New Zealand's defence of the America's Cup. The **iwi** of the *rohe* include Ngati Paoa, Ngati Te Ata, Ngati Akitai, Kawerau a Maki, Ngati Mahuta, Ngai Tai, Ngati Tahinga, Ngati Wai and Ngati Whatua. Auckland itself is the world's largest **Polynesian city**, with around twenty percent of the population either of Maori descent or the families of migrants who arrived from Tonga, Samoa, the Cook Islands and other South Pacific islands during the 1960s and 1970s. For further tourist **information** consult ⓦ www.aucklandnz.com.

Auckland Museum

The Domain ⓦ www.aucklandmuseum.com. Daily 10am–5pm. Admission by $5 donation.

Auckland Museum houses one of the most extensive Maori and Pacific collections in the world, showcasing carvings, tools, textiles, art and domestic implements. The Maori collection is dominated by **Hotunui**, a restored meeting house built in 1878 and re-erected here in 1929. The craftsmanship is superb, both here and on the intricately carved war canoe, **Te Toki a**

Discover New Zealand.

See it all with Air New Zealand. With over 500 flights daily to 26 destinations nationwide, you'll be able to see everything New Zealand has to offer.
For everyday low fares call 0800 737 000 or visit an Air New Zealand Travelcentre.

AIR NEW ZEALAND

Being there is everything

airnewzealand.co.nz

Lake Diamond, Southern Alps.

100% PURE NEW ZEALAND

Race back to the Ice Age with a journey to the South Island's Southern Alps region. From the incredible Passchendaele Icefall to the glistening expanse of the Bonar Glacier, you'll experience a landscape that has barely altered since time began. Explore this ancient land in modern comfort by helicopter, 4-wheel drive or mountain bike. If you're up for an original adventure, it doesn't get much purer than this.

newzealand.com

Falls River, Abel Tasman

EXPERIENCE THE

colours of New Zealand™

**Millennium Hotels and Resorts
invite you to experience New Zealand.**

Relax, indulge and explore New Zealand at any of our 31 hotels located from the Bay of Islands in the North to Dunedin in the South.

Choose total luxury at Millennium, superbly appointed corporate and leisure at Copthorne or experience true 'kiwi' hospitality at Kingsgate.

Enjoy our World of Hospitality.

MILLENNIUM
HOTELS AND RESORTS

MILLENNIUM · COPTHORNE · KINGSGATE

For reservations please phone

New Zealand	0800 808 228
Australia	1 800 124 420
North America	1 866 866 8086
Singapore	65 6735 7575
United Kingdom	0800 41 47 41

www.millenniumhotels.com

Tapiri, the only surviving specimen from the pre-European era. Elsewhere you are bombarded with magnificent work in the shape of store houses and stand-alone statues, many of them the work of carvers from the Rotorua (Arawa) district. In total, there are three floors of exhibition galleries, as well as a vibrant Children's Discovery Centre. A Maori cultural group (see listing below) performs daily, heralded by a conch blast echoing through the halls of the museum.

Auckland Art Gallery

Cnr Wellesley and Kitchener streets
ⓦ www.aucklandartgallery.govt.nz. Daily 10am–5pm. Admission free; also free 45min tours daily at 2pm.

One of New Zealand's finest collections of early colonial art is on display in the Heritage wing of the **Auckland Art Gallery**. Works change frequently, but you can expect to find original drawings by the artists on James Cook's expeditions, as well as romanticised images of Maori life seen through European eyes that contributed to a mythical view that persisted for decades. Much of the rest of the early collection is devoted to works by two of the country's most loved artists, both highly respected by Maori as among the few to portray their ancestors accurately. **Gottfried Lindauer** spent the late 1800s painting lifelike, almost documentary, portraits of *rangatira* (chiefs) and high-born Maori men and women. In the early part of the twentieth century, **Charles F. Goldie** became New Zealand's resident "old master" and earned international recognition for his portraits of elderly Maori subjects regally showing off their traditional *moko* (tattoos).

National Maritime Museum

Cnr Quay and Hobson streets ⓦ www.nzmaritime.org. Daily: Oct–April 9am–6pm, May–Sept 9am–5pm. Admission $12.

For coverage of the maritime and social history of this island

AUCKLAND ART GALLERY

nation it is hard to beat the **National Maritime Museum** on Auckland's waterfront. Maori colonisation is brought to life in the digital, animated *Te Waka* film, which follows an imagined Maori migration voyage, setting the scene for a display of outrigger and double-hulled canoes from all over the South Pacific. The creaking and rolling innards of a migrant ship and displays on New Zealand's coastal traders and whalers illustrate European arrival.

Maungawhau

2km south of the city centre; bus #275 or #277 from Britomart bus depot. Unrestricted entry.

Maungawhau, or Mount Eden as it is commonly known, is the highest volcano (196m) on the Auckland isthmus and provides great views over the inner city to the Hauraki Gulf. Most of the lower slopes are buried under housing, but the grassy upper reaches still show evidence of *kumara* storage pits, terracing and house sites of settlements from the thirteenth to eighteenth century. This important fortified site was eventually abandoned but the large crater is still known as Te Ipu a Mataahou (the food bowl of the god Mataahou).

Maungakiekie

Cornwall Park, Auckland Ⓦ www.cornwallpark.co.nz; accessible from Greenlane Rd, Manukau Rd or Campbell Rd. Daily 7am–dusk. Admission free.

The Auckland volcanic field has 48 volcanoes that have erupted over the past 150,000 years. They are fairly small in world terms, but **Maungakiekie** (183m), or One Tree Hill, is one of the largest in the field and relatively recent, having erupted around 20,000 years ago. It's the most extensively terraced of all the Auckland volcanoes, whose earthworks cover approximately 45 hectares, making Maungakiekie one of the largest *pa* sites in New Zealand. On the cone there are terraces created for living areas, as well as *kumara* storage pits, which would formerly have

MAUNGAWHAU

Auckland – a Maori perspective

Legend records the arrival of the earliest Maori in the region on the **Tamaki isthmus**, the narrowest neck of land between the Waitemata and Manukau harbours. With plentiful catches from two harbours and rich volcanic soils on a wealth of highly defensible volcano-top sites, the land became the prize of numerous battles over the years. With the arrival of the musket-trading Europeans in the Bay of Islands around the beginning of the nineteenth century, the Northland Ngapuhi tribe was able to launch successful raids on the Tamaki Maori, which, combined with the predations of smallpox epidemics, left the region almost uninhabited. This was a significant factor in its selection as the site of the new capital after the signing of the Treaty of Waitangi in 1840 (though Auckland lost its capital status to Wellington in 1865). No wonder then that Auckland is known as **Tamaki Makaurau**, "the maiden with a hundred lovers" – a place desired by all and conquered by many – and this also explains the large number of *iwi* represented in a relatively small geographical location. Today, the Ngati Whatua people are acknowledged as *tangata whenua* (the people of the land) of the Tamaki isthmus and their *marae* (tribal meeting place) occupies Bastion Point, overlooking Waitemata Harbour.

been roofed. The site has ancient paths, which can be seen in several places, and is defended by boundary walls, scarps, ditches and banks. Palisades and fighting stages would have protected the entranceways. An archaeological trail covers the major points of interest (pick up the trail guide at the Information Centre) and there are often guided tours led by an archaeologist.

Otara Market

18km south of central Auckland. Market held Sat 6am–noon, but go early. Take the Otara exit off the southern motorway or catch buses #487 or #497 from Britomart bus depot.

South Auckland is the city's poorest sector and the less-thanflatteringly-depicted gangland setting for Lee Tamahori's film *Once Were Warriors*. It is worth venturing down here for the **Otara Market**, plausibly billed as the largest Maori and Polynesian market in the world. Its authenticity is diluted by market traders selling cheap trinkets, but you'll see island-style floral print fabrics, reasonably priced Maori carvings, and truckloads of cheap fruit and vegetables, including many varieties peculiar to the islands such as taro and yams. There's even a van ingeniously kitted out to produce an ersatz *hangi*.

MAORI CULTURAL EXPERIENCES

Awhina Victoria Park Market, Victoria St ⊤ 09/307 8890. High-quality art by Maori artists.

Kura Contemporary Ethnic Art 188 Quay St ⊤ 09/302 1151, ⓦ www.kuragallery.co.nz. Taking its title from the red feather worn by chiefs, Kura specialises in contemporary Maori art – paintings, sculpture, ceramics, glass, carving and weaving.

Manaia Maori Cultural Performance Auckland Museum ⊤ 09/306 7048, ⓦ www.aucklandmuseum.com. Thirty-minute cultural shows ($15) take place daily (Jan–March at 11am, noon, 1.30pm & 2.30pm; April–Dec 11am, noon & 1.30pm).

Performances include a welcome dance, *poi* dance, stick game, weaponry display and *haka*, and afterwards you're guided through the museum's Maori collection.

Potiki Adventures ⊤ 09/845 5932 or 0800 692 3836, ⓦ www .potikiadventures.co.nz. Maori-led adventure activities including mountain biking, abseiling, snorkelling and kayaking in some of the region's most stunning locations. From $130 per person.

Tamaki Hikoi ⊤ 0800/AUCKLAND, ⓦ www.aucklandnz.com. Maori-led guided walk ($80) around some of Auckland's most iconic and historic landmarks; includes a picnic lunch.

Tainui

The **Tainui** *rohe* covers a band across the North Island encompassing the area south of Auckland down the west coast to Mokau, then inland to include the Waikato, Hauraki Plains and the Coromandel Peninsula. The **iwi** include Tainui, Ngati Paoa, Ngati Tai, Ngati Maru, Ngati Tamatera, Ngati Whanaunga, Waikato and Maniopoto. The land confiscations in this region have been a deep and enduring memory for local Maori and only in recent times has the New Zealand government attempted to address the matter.

Much of the west of the *rohe* is characterised by lush, rich farmlands threaded by the tributaries of the **Waikato River**, which Maori used as a source for food, notably eel, whitebait, freshwater crayfish, mullet and waterfowl. The river was also used as a network for trade and travel, and for spiritual cleansing and healing, and to this day is held in high regard. The Waikato provincial capital, **Hamilton**, is New Zealand's fourth-largest city, though the site was settled by Maori for at least two hundred years before Europeans arrived in the 1830s. Further east the region is more mountainous and bush-cloaked, fringed with beautiful surf and swimming beaches. The **Coromandel Range** runs through the interior, sculpted millions of years ago by volcanic activity into a jagged and contorted skyline, since clothed in dense rainforest. The range is interpreted as a canoe, with Mount Moehau, at the Coromandel Peninsula's northern tip, as its prow, and Mount Te Aroha in the south, bordering Maori-owned land, the legendary burial place of **Tama te Kapua**, the commander of one of the Great Migration canoes, Te Arawa. In the nineteenth century the region saw the North Island's biggest

gold rush and the legacy of those frenetic years in the 1860s and 1870s can still be seen, especially in and around the town of **Thames**. For more **information** on the region consult Ⓦwww.waikatonz.co.nz and Ⓦwww.thecoromandel.com.

Ngaruawahia

State Hwy 1, between Taupiri and Hamilton, 110km south of Auckland.

The region's most culturally significant spot is the small, mostly Maori, town of **Ngaruawahia**. It is here that the King Movement (see box) had its roots, and it was also the scene of the signing of the 1995 Raupatu Land Settlement, whereby the New Zealand government agreed to compensate the Waikato-Tainui people for land confiscated in the 1860s. A couple of traditional events bring Ngaruawahia alive. On Regatta Day (the closest Saturday to March 17), the Turangawaewae Marae hosts a

The King Movement

Before Europeans arrived, Maori loyalty was solely to their immediate family and tribe, but wrangles with settlers led many tribes to discard age-old feuds in favour of a common cause. In 1856, a chief was sought who might unite the disparate tribes against the Europeans. **Te Wherowhero** was chosen as the leader and, taking the title of Potatau I, he established himself at Ngaruawahia – still the heartland of the **King Movement**. The movement was seen as an act of rebellion by the British and in 1858 armed conflict broke out, soon spreading through the central North Island. The King Movement won a notable victory at Gate Pa in the Bay of Plenty, but was eventually overwhelmed. Potatau's successor, Tawhiao, made peace in 1860. The loose coalition of the contemporary King Movement still plays an important role in the country, and the reigning Maori Queen, Te Arikinui Dame Te Atairangikaahu, has been the recipient of many state and royal visits.

public parade of traditional war canoes (*waka taua*) on the Waikato River, with local Maori competing in events like *waka* racing and *waka* hurdling. Mid-May sees the **coronation** of the Maori Queen when tribal representatives from around the country journey to Ngaruawahia to join in the three-day celebrations.

Turangawaewae Marae contains both **Mahingarangi House**, which houses the Maori throne, and **Turongo House**, the official residence of the Maori Queen. However, these can be seen only when the *marae* is being used for a public event – permission should be sought from the *marae* trustees before attempting closer inspection.

Waikato Museum of Art and History

1 Grantham St, Hamilton ⓦ www.waikatomuseum.org.nz. Daily 10am–4.30pm. Free admission, donations welcome.

Situated on the banks of the Waikato River in Hamilton, the **Waikato Museum of Art and History** (Te Whare Taonga o Waikato) presents an ever-changing programme of exhibitions, utilising its own large collection of New Zealand art, cultural artefacts and historical objects. One enduring feature is a section devoted to Tainui culture, with some superb examples of domestic items, woven flax tools, ritual artefacts, and fine examples of wood and stone carving. Pride of place goes to the magnificent Te Winika war canoe, given to the city of Hamilton in 1973 by the Maori Queen. The museum also houses a significant collection of Tainui *taonga* (treasures).

Kawhia

55km south of Raglan.

The small community of **Kawhia** is the site of the Tainui people's first landfall in Aotearoa – and remains their spiritual home. Tradition tells of their arrival from Hawaiki in 1350 aboard the Tainui *waka*. On arrival the *waka* was tied to a *pohutukawa* tree, Tangi te Korowhiti, which still grows on the shores of Kawhia Harbour. The Tainui canoe itself is buried on a grassy knoll in the grounds of the **Maketu Marae**, above the beautifully carved and painted meeting house. The Maori Queen also has a purpose-built residence at the entrance to the *marae* to illustrate the significance of the site. Kawhia Harbour was so bountiful that Maori lived on its shores for centuries, until tribal battles over the rich fishing grounds forced them inland. For a time it was a prosperous port at the gateway to the fertile King Country, but Kawhia is now a sleepy little place firmly in the shadow of the lively surfing town of Raglan, 55km to the north.

Waitomo Glowworm Caves

Waitomo Ⓦ www.waitomocaves.co.nz. Daily (end Oct–Easter Monday) 9am–5.30pm; (winter) 9am–5pm; tours every 30min. Admission $30. For caving trips – from $90 – see Ⓦ www.waitomo.co.nz, Ⓦ www.blackwaterrafting.co.nz and Ⓦ www.caveraft.com.

Maori have long known of the existence of the **Waitomo Glowworm Caves** and it was local chief, Tane Tinorau, who first led English surveyor, Fred Mace, into this labyrinth in 1887. The limestone formations and ceilings flecked with constellations of glowworms were so impressive that Tane was soon guiding tourists into the caves. The government took over operations in 1906 and it wasn't until 1989 that the caves were returned to their traditional Maori owners. They now participate in the site's management and receive a percentage of all the revenue generated from gentle, **underground walking tours**, which culminate with a boat ride through the cave grotto, where glowworms overhead shed pinpricks of ghostly pale-green light. Waitomo also has half a dozen far more adventurous **caving trips** with long abseils and the chance to ride inner tubes down underground rivers.

Kauaeranga Valley

DOC office, Kauaeranga Valley Rd, 13km east of Thames. Daily 8am–4pm, info by email from Ⓔ kauaerangavc@doc.govt.nz.

The **Kauaeranga River**, to the east of the township of

Thames, was once named Waiwhakauaeranga, meaning "waters of the stacked-up jawbones". Ngati Maru historians claim the name originated after a battle, where members of Ngati Maru stacked up the jawbones of their defeated enemies in rows on the banks of the river.

Its steep-sided **valley** stretches towards the spine of the Coromandel Peninsula, a jagged landscape of bluffs and gorges topped by the **Pinnacles** (759m), with breathtaking views to both coasts. The local DOC office has displays on the region's early milling history, and you can stock up on maps and strike off on a range of easily accessible tramps, ranging from a twenty-minute stroll to a two-day circuit with a night spent at the Pinnacles Hut.

MAORI CULTURAL EXPERIENCES

Aotea Horse Trekking
☎ 07/871 0324, ⓦ www.kawhia .maori.nz. Gentle scenic horse rides (3hr, $60) over some lovely scenery around Kawhia Harbour, often led by local Tainui rider and acclaimed show jumper, Vanessa Tuapiki.

Kawhia History Tours
☎ 07/871 0324, ⓦ www.kawhia.maori.nz. The stately 50-year-old *Kawhia*, a former Auckland ferry, has been pressed into use for two-and-a-half-hour harbour cruises (usually daily at 11am and/or 2pm, reservations essential, $35), during which you're regaled with tales of warrior chief Te Rauparaha.

Mokau River Cruises ☎ 06/752 9775, ⓦ www.kawhia.maori.nz. Cruises on the Mokau River, 70km southwest of Waitomo, aboard the 1913 mail-and-dairy boat *MV Cygnet*. Maori tradition hangs heavy here, and Pauline and Grant convey much of this as you cruise by significant spots. Departures daily 11am (Oct–May) weather permitting, $35.

Te Toi Manawa 1007 Kennedy Bay Rd, R.D.3, Coromandel ☎ 07/866 7919, ⓦ www .toimanawa.co.nz. Te Toi Manawa (The Art Beat) stocks contemporary and traditional Maori arts and crafts, and is the outlet for Dr Pakariki Harrison, one of New Zealand's finest master carvers.

Arawa

Mai Maketu ki Tongariro ("from Maketu to Tongariro") is a well-known proverb that denotes the tribal boundaries of the **Arawa** *rohe*. It is said that the bow of the Great Migratory canoe Arawa rests at Maketu and the stern at Tongariro, so the descendants from that canoe live throughout this region. Arawa territory today stretches from Papamoa on the Bay of Plenty coast to Atiamuri on the Waikato River, and east across the Kaingaroa Forest to Matata, where the Tarawera River reaches the sea. The Arawa *rohe* comprises the **iwi** of Te Arawa and Ngati Tuwharetoa.

Prior to the arrival of Europeans, the Rotorua region was famed far and wide for the curative powers of its thermal pools. The naturally hot water lured Maori to settle around **Lake Rotorua** and **Lake Tarawera**, using the hottest pools for cooking and the cooler ones for bathing. In this respect, catering to European visitors, who began to descend in numbers in the early nineteenth century, was simply an extension of an established practice. The first major tourist attraction, the Pink and White Terraces at **Te Wairoa**, on the shores of Lake Tarawera, was destroyed by the eruption of Mount Tarawera in 1886, but local tribes were quick to grasp the commercial possibilities as **Rotorua** itself expanded into a spa town in the late nineteenth century. There is still no better place today to get an introduction to Maori values, traditions, song and dance than at one of the concert and *hangi* evenings held all over the so-called "Sulphur City" of Rotorua. Meanwhile, for Maori, who see themselves as *kaitiaki* (guardians) of the geothermal resources, the region's natural features continue to hold a spiritual significance. For example, at **Whakarewarewa** – one of several original Maori settlements in the Rotorua area – there are names for each of the 189 pools, and each has its individual story.

South of Rotorua, **Whirinaki Forest Park** forms a boundary between the Kaingaroa Forest to the west and Te Urewera National Park to the east. Yet further south, **Lake Taupo** draws anglers and holidaymakers to its deep waters, while the volcanic peaks of the **Tongariro National Park** attract hikers, skiers and *Lord of the Rings* fans. For more regional **information** see Ⓦwww.rotoruanz.com and Ⓦwww.laketauponz.com.

Rotorua Museum

Government Gardens, Rotorua Ⓦwww.rotoruamuseum.co.nz. Daily: Oct–March 9am–8pm, April–Sept 9am–5pm. Admission $11.

The neo-Tudor bathhouse that was once the centrepiece of Rotorua's spa treatment industry is now home to the town's principal museum, also known as **Te Whare Taonga O Te Arawa**. The small but significant Te Arawa collection showcases the long-respected talents of Arawa carvers, whose magnificent figures, *pounamu* (greenstone) weapons and intricate *maihi* (barge boards) are all powerfully presented. Prized pieces include the flute supposedly played by the legendary lover Tutanekai, an unusually fine pumice goddess, and rare eighteenth-century carvings executed with stone (rather than metal) tools.

St Faith's Anglican Church

Ohinemutu, central Rotorua. Open daylight hours. Admission by donation.

The lakeside Maori village of **Ohinemutu** pre-dates the town of Rotorua that has grown up around it. Ohinemutu remains an overwhelmingly Maori village, centred on its hot springs and the small wooden **St Faith's Anglican Church**, built in 1914. The

Hinemoa and Tutanekai

Mokoia Island, in Lake Rotorua, is the setting for the story of **Hinemoa and Tutanekai**, the greatest of all Maori love stories. Hinemoa's family forbade her from marrying the island's young chief, Tutanekai, and prevented her from meeting him by beaching their *waka*, but the strains of Tutanekai's flute wafted across the lake nightly and the smitten Hinemoa resolved to swim to him. Buoyed by gourds, she set off but by the time she reached the island, Tutanekai had returned to his house to sleep. Without clothes, Hinemoa was unable to enter the village so she immersed herself in a hot pool. Presently, Tutanekai's slave came to collect water, and Hinemoa lured him over, smashed his gourd and sent him back to his master. An enraged Tutanekai came to investigate, only to fall into Hinemoa's embrace.

church's neo-Tudor exterior gives no hint of the gloriously rich interior where there is barely a patch of wall that hasn't been carved or covered with *tukutuku* (ornamental latticework panels). Everything has been intricately worked, from pew ends and support beams to the entrance to the chancel, which has been made to look like the *maihi* (barge boards) of a meeting house. Even the pulpit has been inlaid with geometrically patterned cloth. Wonderful though all this is, most people come to see the figure of Christ, swathed in a Maori cloak and feathers, etched into a window positioned so that he appears to be walking on the lake.

Te Puia

State Hwy 5, 3km south of central Rotorua ⓦ www.tepuia.com. Daily 8am–5pm. Admission $25; free hour-long guided tours leave on the hour.

Part of the Whakarewarewa thermal valley falls under the auspices of **Te Puia**, where a series of walkways thread past pools of boiling mud, sulphurous springs, agglomerations of silica stalactites and the prolific twenty-metre Pohutu ("big splash") geyser. It is an extraordinary landscape, especially in winter when the steam condenses into thick clouds.

The complex also includes a replica of a traditional **Maori village** – its entrance marked by a carving of lovers Tutanekai and Hinemoa embracing – and the **Maori Arts and Crafts Institute**, which serves both to teach young Maori traditional carving and weaving techniques and to demonstrate those same skills to visitors. Half an hour spent here can be wonderfully inspirational, as skilled artisans produce flax skirts and carvings, which can be bought in the classy but expensive shop.

Te Whakarewarewa Thermal Village

Tyron St, 3km south of central Rotorua. Daily 8.30am–5pm.
Admission $20; free cultural performances at 11.15am & 2pm.

The northern section of the Whakarewarewa thermal area can be visited at **Te Whakarewarewa Thermal Village**, which unlike the other thermal areas is a living village. The Ngati Wahiao and Tuhourangi people have lived here since being displaced by the 1886 eruption of Mount Tarawera. You can't get really close to the geysers, but there is considerable compensation in being able to wander around the houses, many of them fairly new constructions, as the hydrogen sulphide issuing from the ground tends to rot concrete. You might even see people using steam boxes for cooking, and can sample geothermally cooked food from the sweetcorn stand near the entrance. Assorted souvenir shops demonstrate carving and weaving skills, while you can also partake in a *hangi* (served at noon; $30).

Okere Falls Scenic Reserve

21km north of Rotorua on Trout Pool Rd, off State Hwy 33.

The **Okere River** – "the place of drifting" – is a significant Maori cultural and spiritual site, highly valued for centuries. Rich in resources, it is the traditional river of Te Arawa *hapu* (sub-tribe) Ngati Pikiao, who fought countless historic battles to guard the waterway's important food sources. The river's other name, Kaituna (*kai* = food, *tuna* = eels), reflects this significance, while it also supplied rushes used in traditional *rongoa* (medicines) and raw materials for weaving and other crafts.

The **Okere Falls Scenic Reserve** is best visited along a broad track (2.5km return; 40min–1hr) passing glimpses of the churning river below and a viewing platform that's perfect for observing rafters plummet over the seven-metre Tutea's Falls. From here, steps descend through short tunnels in the steep rock walls beside the waterfall to **Tutea's Caves**, used as a safe haven during attacks by rival groups.

Tikitere – Hell's Gate

Tikitere, State Hwy 30, 15km northeast of Rotorua
Ⓦ www.hellsgate.co.nz. Daily 8.30am–8.30pm. Admission $20, spa activities (thermal and mud baths, massage, etc) from $70.

Though the least-visited and smallest of Rotorua's major thermal areas, **Hell's Gate** is also the most active and of major importance to the Ngati Rangiteaorere *hapu*. They know the place as **Tikitere**, a name dating back 650 years to a time when the young princess Hurutini cast herself into a boiling pool to remove the shame of her abusive and disrespectful husband. Her mother found her dead body and lamented "aue e teri nei tiki" (here lies my precious one – Tikitere). Paths at the reserve lead past steaming fumaroles and pools of boiling mud, then you can retire to the **Wai Ora Spa** for a mud bath, sulphurous spa and massage.

Te Wairoa Buried Village

Tarawera Rd, 15km southeast of Rotorua
Ⓦ www.buriedvillage.co.nz. Daily: Nov–March 8.30am–5.30pm, April–Oct 9am–4.30pm. Admission $22.

The partly excavated and heavily reconstructed remains of **Te Wairoa Buried Village** occupy a lakeside site first established as a Maori settlement by missionaries in 1848 and later used as a staging post for trips to the famed Pink and White Terraces. The 1886 eruption of Mount Tarawera that destroyed the Terraces left the village under three metres of ash. Though excavated since the 1930s, the site has less of a feel of an archaeological dig than that of a manicured orchard: half-buried *whare* (houses) and the foundations of the *Rotomahana Hotel* sit primly on mown lawns among European fruit trees gone to seed, marauding hawthorn and a perfect row of full-grown poplars fostered by a line of fence posts. The site's museum does a great job of capturing both the spirit of the village in its heyday and the aftermath of its destruction, through numerous photographs and various ash-encrusted knick-knacks.

Tongariro National Park

DOC Visitor Centre, Whakapapa Village, 50km south of Lake Taupo, State Hwy 48; for information look under "National Parks" at Ⓦ www.doc.govt.nz.

One of the world's earliest national parks, and New Zealand's first, **Tongariro National Park** was created in 1887 when paramount Ngati Tuwharetoa chief Te Heuheu Tukino IV (Horonuku) donated the sacred peaks of Tongariro (1967m), conical Ngauruhoe (2287m) and broad-shouldered Ruapehu (2797m) to the nation. The gift recognised the region's cultural and spiritual importance to the *tangata whenua* ("people of the land") for whom the mountains are a vital part of their history and their genealogy. To the local Tuwharetoa people these mountains were so sacred that they averted their eyes while passing, honouring their ancestor Ngatoroirangi, who came to claim the centre of the island. After declaring Tongariro *tapu* he set off up the mountain, but his followers broke their vow to fast while he was away. The angry gods sent a snowstorm in which Ngatoroirangi almost perished, before more benevolent gods in Hawaiki saved him by sending fire to revive his frozen limbs – fire that left a trail of vol-canic vents across the land.

Most visitors head straight for the main body of the park, dominated by the three great volcanoes. Barren lava flows, winter snowfields, hot springs and active craters can be seen side by side, while the park's flora varies from alpine herbs to thick swathes of flax, and from the hardy, low-growing shrubs of the Rangipo gravel-field to dense beech forests. The park is known for its two supremely rewarding hikes – the one-day **Tongariro Crossing** and the three- to four-day **Tongariro Northern Circuit**, one of New Zealand's nine "Great Walks".

MAORI CULTURAL EXPERIENCES

Elite Tour Adventures ☎07/347 8282, Ⓦwww.tour-guide.co.nz. Small group tours of Rotorua with the emphasis on geothermal processes, Maori history and legends, flora and fauna. Half-day $100 (including admissions), full day $165.

Kaitiaki Adventures ☎0800 338 736, Ⓦwww.kaitiaki.co.nz. Somehow the *karakia* (prayers) to the river gods seem appropriate as you prepare to raft the Kaituna River with its seven-metre Tutea's Falls. Rafting $75, whitewater sledging $130.

Mana Adventures ☎07/346 8595, Ⓦwww.manaadventures .co.nz. Rental kayaks on Lake Rotorua (half-day $35, full day $55), overnight trips to Mokoia Island ($120), and lake cruises in a purpose-built traditional canoe with Maori guide (from $20).

Mount Tarawera NZ ☎07/349 3714, Ⓦwww.mt-tarawera .co.nz. See sacred Mount Tarawera on a half-day guided 4WD tour ($121) which climbs to the summit, allowing time for a walk (or run) down into the crater. Also helicopter summit landings and fly-drive tours from $415.

Rock 'n' River ☎07/386 0352, Ⓦwww.raftingnewzealand.com. Combine Maori hospitality with adventurous rafting trips on the scenic Tongariro River ($95) or wild Rangitikei River ($99). Also easier half-day self-guided kayak trips on local lakes and streams ($40).

Realm of Tane ℡ 07/346 2823, 🌐 www.maoriculture.co.nz. Dramatic blend of guided tour, theatre and storytelling within a series of indoor sets including a meeting house entrance and native garden. Hour-long tours twice daily, price $30.

Tamaki Maori Village ℡ 07/346 2823, 🌐 www.maoriculture .co.nz. Most popular of Rotorua's out-of-town *hangi*-and-concert combos where visitors are driven out to a specially built "Maori village" 15km south of Rotorua for a spine-chilling welcome. Adults $92.42, children $52.02.

The 8 Beating Hearts ℡ 07/349 1515, 🌐 www.nzmaoritourism .com. Adventure and mainstream tours for small groups accompanied by a Maori guide. Prices from $300 per person for a full 14hr-day, including site admissions.

Wairakei Terraces ℡ 07/378 0913, 🌐 www.wairakeiterraces .co.nz. This attempt to re-create the famed Pink and White Terraces at the Wairakei thermal field (10km north of Taupo, junction of SH1 & SH5) comes combined with a Maori cultural performance. Daily Oct–March 9am–5pm, April–Sept 9am–4.30pm, admission $18, cultural show 6–8.30pm, $75.

Whirinaki Rainforest Guided Walks ℡ 07/377 2363, 🌐 www.rainforest-treks.co.nz. The Ngati Whare and Tuhoe tribes offer cultural walking tours among the tall trees and rushing rivers of Whirinaki Forest Park (100km southeast of Rotorua). One-day walks ($155) operate year-round; three-day treks ($745) are restricted to the summer season (Oct–April).

MAORI CULTURAL EXPERIENCES

Mataatua

The *rohe* of **Mataatua** embraces what is commonly known as the Bay of Plenty, the sweeping bite out of the North Island's northeast coast. It centres on the prosperous port city of **Tauranga** ("safe anchorage") and its beachside acolyte, **Mount Maunganui** (Mauao in Maori), while further east **Whakatane** is the departure point for boat excursions to volcanic **White Island**. The *rohe* draws its name from the Mataatua (the face of God) canoe, or *waka*, that was part of the legendary Great Migration of canoes from Hawaiki. The local **iwi** include Ngati Ranginui, Ngaiterangi, Ngati Pukenga, Ngati Awa, Tuhoe, Whakatohea, Ngati Tai and Te Whanau a Apanui.

European settlement began in 1834 when a mission house was built at Tauranga, whose natural harbour was the logical location for pioneer settlers to disembark from ships and make their way inland to begin their new life. Early European dispersion was slowed by land wars with the Maori in the 1860s, and military bases were quickly established. In 1864 Tauranga was the scene of the bloody **Battle of Gate Pa**, when the government sent troops to prevent supplies and reinforcements from reaching the followers of the King Movement. Most of the local Ngaiterangi hurried back from the Waikato and challenged the soldiers from a *pa* they quickly built near an entrance to the mission land, which became known as Gate Pa. Although they pounded it with artillery, the British lost about a third of their assault force and at nightfall the Ngaiterangi slipped through the British lines to fight again in the Waikato. When the conflicts ended the military bases developed into towns to service the growing numbers of settlers, many of whom were former soldiers. Great areas of forest were burned and cleared to create pastoral farms, and Maori started to move from their traditional village settlements to be nearer the towns. Today, visual evidence of early Maori settlement and habitation is mostly confined to the hilltops and peninsulas around the harbour and throughout the surrounding area. For further regional **information** see ⓦ www.visitplenty.co.nz.

Mauao

7km northeast of Tauranga.

Mauao, or Mount Maunganui, at the eastern entrance to Tauranga Harbour, is the most sacred landmark in the Tauranga area. According to oral tradition it was once a nameless hill, the *pononga* or slave to a majestic mountain called Otanewainuku. The nameless one desired the heart of a nearby hill called Puwhenua, adorned in the many different colours and shades of Tane Mahuta, the God of the Forest, but Puwhenua's heart had already been won by Otanewainuku. So in deep despair he decided to drown himself, calling upon his friends to help him, the Patupaiarehe (fairy people), who dwelt in the dark recesses of the forest and possessed magical powers. When night fell they embraced the nameless one with ropes, wrenching him from his standing place, carving a valley as they pulled him towards Te Moananui-a-Kiwa (the Pacific Ocean). As the Patupaiarehe approached the ocean, having lost track of time, the sun began to creep slowly over the horizon. The Patupaiarehe melted away and left the nameless one at the place that he now stands, where he became known as Mauao ("caught by the dawn").

Ngati Ranginui and Waitaha were the original inhabitants of Mauao, building an immense fortified village on the mountain. Ngaiterangi *iwi* conquered the mountain in around 1700, though they abandoned it following the murder of a large number of their people there in 1820. Mauao then became a *wahi tapu* (sacred area) and subsequently the three *iwi* of

Tauranga, the Ngaiterangi, Ngati Ranginui and Ngati Pukenga, have resisted any commercial development on the mountain. The same can't be said of the vibrant beach resort of **Mount Maunganui**, which huddles beneath the extinct volcanic cone of the mountain. "The Mount", as hill and town are often known, was once an island but is now connected to the mainland by a narrow neck of dune sand covered with apartments, shops, restaurants and houses.

Whakatane

80km southeast of Tauranga. Museum and gallery at 11 Boon St Ⓦ www.whakatanemuseum.org.nz. Mon–Fri 10am–4.30pm, Sat & Sun 11am–3pm.

Whakatane (meaning "act like a man") is sometimes known as the birthplace of Aotearoa, for it was here that the Polynesian navigator Toi te Huatahi first landed. Despite being the main settlement of the eastern Bay of Plenty, Whakatane is a small town, its centre built around its defining feature, a large rock called **Pohaturoa** ("long rock"). The outcrop is sacred to Maori and the small park surrounding the rock contains a black marble monument to Te Hurinui Apanui, a great chief who propounded the virtues of peace and is mourned by Pakeha and Maori alike. This site was once a shrine where rites were performed by Maori priests, and the seed that grew into the *karaka* trees at the base of the rock are said to have arrived on the Mataatua canoe.

Maori *taonga* (treasures) from the local *iwi*, tracing their descent from the Mataatua canoe, are on display at the **Whakatane Museum and Gallery**, which also features well-conceived displays on geological matters and European colonial history.

White Island

50km north of Whakatane. Boat trips (6hr, $150) with PeeJay Charters Ⓣ 07/308 9588, Ⓦ www.whiteisland.co.nz.

Uninhabited **White Island** (Te Puia o Whaakari) lies stranded in the Bay of Plenty, where Cook came across it and named it for its permanent shroud of steam from the active crater. To vulcanologists it is no more or less than New Zealand's only live marine volcano, but in Maori lore it was created when the priest Ngatoroirangi called up fire to warm his freezing limbs when stranded on Mount Tongariro. On its way from the Maori homelands in Hawaiki the fire occasionally broke through the surface, first here at White Island. Visitors flock here to appreciate its desolate landscape of sulphur-yellow crystal deposits, billowing towers of gas, and a crater lake 60m below sea level.

St Stephen's Church

Church St, Opotiki, 60km east of Whakatane. Key available from Opotiki Museum.

The innocent-looking white clapboard **St Stephen's Church**, set among trees full of chirruping birds, was once the scene of a

---

Te Kooti Rikirangi

Te Kooti Rikirangi was one of the most celebrated of Maori "rebels", a thorn in the side of the colonial government throughout the New Zealand Wars of the late 1860s and early 1870s. Depicted in European schoolbooks as a ruthless guerrilla leader and the wildest outlaw in Maori history, in truth he was a mild-mannered man with a neatly trimmed beard and moustache rather than the more confrontational *moko* (traditional tattoos). An excellent fighter and brilliant strategist, Te Kooti kept the mountainous spine of North Island on edge for the best part of a decade, eluding the biggest manhunt in New Zealand's history. With the end of the wars in 1872, Te Kooti took refuge in the Maori safe haven of the King Country. He was eventually pardoned in 1883, and in 1891 was granted a plot of land near Whakatane, where he lived out the last two years of his life.

notorious murder. It was here in March 1865, in the Bay of Plenty's easternmost settlement, that local missionary and church builder Carl Völkner was allegedly killed by Kereopa Te Rau, a leader of the revivalist Hau Hau movement, which rejected zealous Christianity in favour of a synthesis of Old Testament and Maori beliefs. The case is far from clear-cut, however: at the time, many Maori believed that missionaries doubled as spies, duly reporting their findings to the settlers and military, and it appears that Völkner had indeed written many letters to Governor Grey espousing settlers' land-grabbing ambitions. Local Maori claim Völkner was justly executed after being confronted with the evidence and denounced as a traitor. Whatever the truth, the settlers used the story as propaganda, fuelling intermittent skirmishes over the next three years. Inside the church, gorgeous *tukutuku* (woven panels) surround the altar beside Völkner's grave.

MAORI CULTURAL EXPERIENCES

Action Stations ☎07/574 9622, ⓦ www.actionstations.co.nz. Mount Maunganui-based small-group tour company specialising in custom-designed eco-tours – choose your itinerary, from half-day trips to multi-day inclusive packages.

Motu River Jet Boat Tours ☎07/315 8107. Jetboat trips up the lower reaches of the Motu River, near Opotiki, with the emphasis on the area's history and culture – 30min spins ($40) to a 2hr exploration ($100).

Paparoa Marae Tourism ☎07/552 5904. The traditional *wero* (challenge) and *hongi* (greeting) precede a visit to the meeting house, where the carvings and oral traditions are explained. The *marae* is 15km west of Tauranga and offers four separate packages (1–3hr, $25–55 per person).

Tauranga Marine Charters ☎07/552 6283, ⓦ www .taurangamarinecharters.co.nz. Maori-owned and operated fishing boat charters taking visitors bottom-fishing for *tarakihi* and snapper. $90 gets you a full day out, rod and bait.

Tairawhiti

Tairawhiti – "the coast upon which the sun shines across the water" – is located on the east coast of the North Island. Its geographical boundaries stretch from the East Cape to Lake Waikaremoana in the west, and Whangara (film location for *Whalerider*) in the south. Local **iwi** include the Ngati Porou, Rongowhakaata and Te Atinga-a-Mahaki.

Contemporary Maori, who make up a significant percentage of the *rohe*'s population (and own over eighty percent of the land), draw on their culture to cope with the hardships of the untamed landscape. The Pacific Coast Highway (SH35) runs for 330 scenic kilometres around the **East Cape** peninsula, hugging the rugged coastline much of the way and passing through a series of Maori towns and villages that present a side of New Zealand seldom seen by tourists. Inland, the inhospitable Waiapu Mountains encompass the northeastern Raukumara Range and the typical native flora of the **Raukumara Forest Park**. The rugged peaks of Hikurangi, Whanokao, Aroangi, Wharekia and Tatai provide a spectacular backdrop to the coastal scenery, but are only accessible through Maori land and permission must be sought by hikers. Similarly isolated, but with open access, is the spectacular **Te Urewera National Park**, encompassing **Lake Waikaremoana**, surrounded by the wonderful Lake Waikaremoana Track.

The region also holds a special place in the European history of New Zealand. In October 1769 **Captain James Cook** first set foot on Aotearoa and immediately ran into conflict with local Maori, killing several before sailing away empty-handed. He named the landing site **Poverty Bay**, because he went away with nothing, though contemporary Maori have sought to rename the area Turanganui-a-Kiwa ("the stopping place of Kiwa"), in honour of a Polynesian navigator. European settlement began in earnest in 1831 with the establishment of the provincial capital, **Gisborne**, which was named after a British Colonial Secretary. For further regional **information**, consult Ⓦ www.gisbornenz.com.

St Mary's Church

Tikitiki, State Hwy 35, 145km north of Gisborne. Daily 9am–5pm. Admission $5, guided tour $15.

The small, wooden Anglican **St Mary's Church**, beside the highway in the minor East Cape village of Tikitiki, looks modest enough, but its plain exterior hides a treasure trove of elaborate and fine Maori design, *tukutuku* (woven panels) and carving. Unusually, the stained glass also utilises Maori designs, while the rafters come painted in the colours of a Maori meeting house.

Mount Hikurangi

Raukumara Forest Park, 80km north of Gisborne. For track access permission, contact Te Runanga o Ngati Porou Ⓣ06/867 9960; for 4WD tours, see listing below.

At 1754m, **Mount Hikurangi** is the highest non-volcanic peak on the North Island and crowns the Raukumara Range. Its summit is the first point on mainland New Zealand to see the sun rise each day: a spectacular sight. It is also a very spiritual mountain for local Ngati Porou; according to oral tradition, when Maui fished up Aotearoa from the depths of the ocean, he first hauled up Hikurangi, leaving his canoe, Nukutaimemeha, stranded on its peak. Tribal tradition states that Nukutaimemeha still rests in petrified form on top of the mountain. The mountain is part of **Raukumara Forest Park**, and exhibits the northernmost examples of alpine vegetation along with stands of beech and *rimu*. A hiking trail (sometimes closed) from Tapuaeroa Road leads across Ngati Porou land to an overnight hut (4–6hr one-way; $15) and on to the summit (1–2hr further).

Cook Landing Site National Historic Reserve

Kaiti Beach, central Gisborne. Unrestricted access.

Landscaped grounds surround a 1906 granite monument at **Cook Landing Site National Historic Reserve**, a pivotal location in the history of both Maori and Pakeha. It was here, just east of the Turanganui River mouth on October 9, 1769, that the crew of **Captain James Cook**'s ship *Endeavour* became the first Europeans to view the east coast of Aotearoa. Local Maori perceived the ship and its longboats as an enormous and beautiful bird surrounded by fledglings, while Cook and his shipmates were thought to be *atua* (gods). As Cook and some of his men were walking along Waikanae Stream, they heard gunfire and returned to discover a Maori had been killed while warning shots were being fired. The following day the Rongowhakaata people challenged a landing party with a *haka* and Cook and a Maori leader met to exchange gifts. When a sword was snatched, a shot was fired and another Maori was fatally wounded. Further misunderstandings led to more Maori deaths, but some Maori were still welcomed aboard the *Endeavour* for food and gifts, some even spending the night. After three nights Cook sailed from Poverty Bay, named by Cook "...as it afforded us no one thing we wanted".

Titirangi

Titirangi Domain, Gisborne. Unrestricted access.

Right next to Cook's landing site is the 130-metre-high **Titirangi** (Kaiti Hill), which, according to local tradition, was the point of arrival of the migratory *waka*, Horouta, which brought the first Maori to the area. From the summit, sentries got matchless views over land and sea. The well-watered folds and flatlands below made for fertile gardens, but the area had been abandoned before Cook arrived. The hill is now surmounted by a lookout and a statue of Cook.

Tairawhiti Museum

18 Stout St, Gisborne Ⓦ www.tairawhitimuseum.org.nz.
Christmas–Jan daily 10am–4pm, Feb–Christmas Mon–Fri
10am–4pm & Sat–Sun 1.30–4pm. Admission by donation.

Located on the banks of the Waimata River, the **Tairawhiti Museum** contains extensive displays on East Coast Maori, with a particularly strong showing of contemporary Maori arts including beautiful *kete* (flax baskets), and greenstone finely carved into *tiki* (pendants). Heritage exhibits include material on Cook's arrival, the role of shipping and coastal wrecks, while outside the museum stands six-room **Wyllie Cottage** (1872), the oldest extant house in town, and the **Sled House**, built on runners so that it could be hauled away by a team of bullocks at the first sign of unrest.

Te Poho o Rawiri

Queens Rd, Kaiti, Gisborne. Visits by arrangement, call ☏ 06/868 5364.

On the eastern side of Titirangi lies **Te Poho o Rawiri**, a *marae* containing one of the largest and most important *whare rununga* (meeting houses) in the country. The current *whare* – built on the site of others dating back to the mid-nineteenth century – was constructed in 1930 and the interior is superb. It is almost completely covered in fine ancestor carvings, interspersed with wonderfully varied geometric *tukutuku* (woven panels). At the foot of the two support poles, ancient and intricately carved warrior statues provide a fine counterpoint to the bolder work on the walls. The *tekoteko* (human figure), kneeling on the right knee with the right hand held upwards, represents Rawiri Te Eke Tu A Terangi, the ancestor who challenges those who enter the *marae*. This is one of the most easily accessible working *marae*, but it is still necessary to arrange permission to enter the site, preferably a day or two beforehand, and a *koha* (donation) is appreciated.

Te Urewera National Park

State Hwy 38, 67km northwest of Wairoa, 160km southeast of Rotorua. For horse trekking, see listing below.

Te Urewera National Park straddles the North Island's mountainous backbone and encompasses the largest untouched expanse of native bush outside of Fiordland on the South Island. Even the highest peaks – some approaching 1500m – barely poke through a dense cloak of primeval forest whose undergrowth is trampled by deer and wild pigs. One road, SH38, penetrates the interior, but the way to get a true sense of the place is to go tramping around the steep-sided Lake Waikaremoana (see below), at the southern end of the park.

From pre-colonial days the Urewera has been home to the **Tuhoe** people, the "Children of the Mist", who learned to live in harmony with this challenging environment. They still live in the interior of the park, the largest concentration around the tramping base of **Ruatahuna**. This was also home to Maori prophet, Rua Kenana, who in 1906 established a religious group at Maungapohatu, where his disciples cleared bush for the raising of sheep and cattle. Rua is remembered for his ability to bring prosperity to the Urewera and, by encouraging Maori to sell land to the Crown, was instrumental in keeping the park in its unspoiled state.

Lake Waikaremoana

State Hwy 38, 67km northwest of Wairoa, 160km southeast of Rotorua (regular bus service). DOC visitor centre at Aniwaniwa. For information follow "National Parks" link from ⓦ www.doc.govt.nz.

The magnificent, bush-girt **Lake Waikaremoana** – highlight

How Lake Waikaremoana was formed

Legend tells that long ago **Lake Waikaremoana** was created by the work of Haumapuhia, the recalcitrant daughter of Maahu, who was drowned by her father and turned into a *taniwha* (water spirit). In a frenzied effort to get to the sea, she charged in every direction, thereby creating the various arms of the lake. As she frantically ran south towards Onepoto, the dawn caught her, turning her to stone at a spot where the lake is said to ripple from time to time, in a watery memory of her titanic struggle.

of Te Urewera National Park – fills a huge scalloped bowl precariously held back by the Panekiri and Ngamoko ranges. The lake came into being around 2200 years ago when a huge bank of sandstone boulders was dislodged from the Ngamoko Range, blocking the river that once drained the valleys and thereby forming the lake. Maori, however, have a more poetic explanation of the lake's creation (see box). The lake has few facilities – one of its attractions – with just a DOC visitor centre and motor camp set up to cater for walkers. Other camping areas and picnic spots are signposted around the lake. On a short visit you can see the **Papakorito Falls**, 2km east of the visitor centre, though walk leaflets are available for longer tramps such as the renowned **Lake Waikaremoana Track**. This is among the finest four-day walks in the country, encircling the "Sea of Rippling Waters" and passing deep clear waters fringed by white sandy beaches and rocky bluffs, making it ideal for swimming, diving, fishing and kayaking.

MAORI CULTURAL EXPERIENCES

Dive Tatapouri ☎ 06/868 5153, ⓦ www.divetatapouri.com. The nearest operator to the Te

Tapuwae o Rongokako Marine Reserve (16km north of Gisborne). From $80 per person for diving and fishing, plus $20 a night for backpacker-style accommodation.

East Cape Fishing Charters
℡ 06/864 4694,
ⓦ www.eastcapefishing.co.nz. Based in secluded Onepoto Bay, offering fishing charters promoting Maori *tikanga* (customary fishing practice) to ensure sustainability (half a day for up to five people, $280). Also three-hour dolphin watching trips (minimum three people, $55 per person).

Eastender Farmstay Tikitiki
℡ 06/864 3820. Touted as the first farm to see the sun, this backpacker-style camp offers simple accommodation (camping $10, backpacker $20) and horse treks ($55).

Gisborne Hotel Gisborne
℡ 06/868 4109,
ⓦ www.gisbornehotel.com. All the art inside the hotel is original and the staff are Maori, while outside special flaxes and native trees have been planted. B&B from $120 for two. Trudy conducts local tours (3hr, $150) to her *marae*, Rongopai, built by her grandfather and others.

Mahana Gallery ℡ 06/864 8878. Arts and crafts gallery in the Maori town of Ruatoria, 130km north of Gisborne, with contemporary and traditional work by local Ngati Porou.

Mt Hikurangi Guided 4WD Tribal Tours ℡ 021/676 910, ⓦ www.ngatiporou.iwi.nz. 4WD tours (4–6hr, $60) on Ngati Porou's sacred mountain, run by Ngati Porou people themselves.

Te Urewera Adventures of NZ ℡ 07/366 3969. Wilderness horse trekking in the heart of Te Urewera National Park with the Tuhoe, from one day in the Whakatane Valley ($117) to three-day trips ($585) staying in semi-permanent bush camps. They also run three-day guided tramping trips (Nov–March only, $408).

Whale Rider Tours ℡ 06/868 5878,
ⓔ heemitaumaunu@xtra.co.nz. Three-hour guided tours ($50) from Gisborne to Whangara (30km northeast) to see where the movie *Whalerider* was filmed. The tour includes visiting the house where much of the filming took place and talking to one of the film's cultural advisors.

MAORI CULTURAL EXPERIENCES

Takitimu

The **Takitimu** *rohe* stretches from the Wairoa district (in modern-day Hawke's Bay) right down the east coast of the North Island to Cape Palliser in the Wairarapa region. The *rohe* name is that of one of the *waka* that brought the Maori people from Hawaiki to Aotearoa, and the local **iwi** include Ngati Kahungunu, Rangitane, Ngati Tama, Ngati Mutunga, Te Ati Awa, Rongomaiwahine, Rongowhakaata, Te Aitanga a Mahaki and Ta Manuhiri. The earliest Maori arrivals travelled down the coast from the north, landing at Wairoa, the Ahuriri lagoon and at Waimarama, and settled in the river valleys and along the coast where food was plentiful. In the sixteenth century, Taraia, great-grandson of the great Kahungunu, established the large tribe of Ngati Kahungunu, which eventually colonised the entire eastern side of the North Island from Poverty Bay to Wairarapa. This *iwi* still lays claim to ownership of the lion's share of the *rohe*.

In 1769, Captain Cook sailed past Ahuriri, the current site of **Napier**, noting its superb saltwater lagoon – the only substantial sheltered mooring between Gisborne and Wellington. He anchored off what came to be known as **Cape Kidnappers**, on account of a less-than-cordial encounter with the Ngati Kahungunu people. Some thirty years later, when early whalers followed in Cook's tracks, Ahuriri was all but deserted, the Ngati Kahungunu having been driven out by rivals equipped with guns. During the uneasy peace of the early colonial years, Maori returned to the Napier area which weathered the land wars of the 1860s relatively unscathed and profited from the relative peace. Long dubbed the "fruit bowl" of New Zealand, it's famed for its orchards, though in recent years the torch has passed to grapes, making the Napier and Hastings area one of the country's foremost **wine regions**. For further **information** consult Ⓦ www.hawkesbaynz.co.nz.

Hawke's Bay and Cape Kidnappers

Gannet Beach Adventures Ⓦ www.gannets.com. Four-hour tours, daily Oct to early May, $30.

The Maori legend of the creation of Aotearoa sees Maui the demigod using a magic jawbone to fish up the North Island. That jawbone remained and now forms **Hawke's Bay**. When Captain Cook visited the area in 1769, a group of Maori in canoes came out to the *Endeavour* to trade. Seeing two young Tahitian interpreters aboard the ship, and believing them to be held against their will, the traders captured one of them and paddled away. The Tahitian escaped back to the ship, but Cook subsequently marked the point on his chart as **Cape Kidnappers**.

Neither James Cook nor Joseph Banks, both meticulous in recording flora and fauna, mentioned the presence of any gannets on the cape. However, a hundred years later, twenty or so pairs were recorded, and now there are over five thousand pairs – making the cape the world's largest mainland **gannet colony**. Best viewed from early November to late February, the gannets can be visited on several tours, the original and cheapest being by tractor-hauled trailer along the beach. Alternatively you can walk there at low tide from Clifton (11km; 5hr return).

Te Mata Peak

5km southeast of Havelock North.

Driving from Hastings to Havelock North, the long ridge of limestone bluffs that make up the 399-metre **Te Mata Peak**

Pokarekare Ana

If there is one song that brings a tear to the eye of homesick Kiwis it is **Pokarekare Ana**. This love song – originally written around 1917 – gained international exposure when first performed by opera singer Kiri Te Kanawa and has more recently cropped up on Hayley Westenra's album, *Pure*. Though it probably had earlier roots, the song was fashioned into its current form by Paraire Tomoana from Waipatu in Hawke's Bay for his fiancée, Kuini Ripeka Ryland from Tokomaru Bay on the East Cape. The song became popular throughout the land, especially among the Te Arawa people who changed the word Waiapu to Rotorua. It goes something like this...

Pokarekare ana
Nga wai on Waiapu
Whiti atu koe hine
Marino ana e
E hine e
Hoki mai ra
Ka mate ahau
I te aroha e

How placid are the ripples
Of restless Waiapu
Dear, they know of your returning
From far across the sea
Dear heart of mine
I'll wait for thee
My love is thine alone
To eternity

looms into view. The ridge is held to be the supine form of a Maori chief, Te Mata O Rongokako, who choked on a rock as he tried to eat through the hill – just one of many Herculean feats with which he attempted to woo the beautiful daughter of a Heretaunga chief. The long and winding Te Mata Peak Road climbs the hill to a wonderful vantage point overlooking the fertile plains, north across Hawke's Bay and Cape Kidnappers, and east to the surf-pounded strands of Ocean Beach and Waimarama, the main swimming beaches for Hastings and Havelock North.

The world's longest place name

44km south of Waipukurau, southern Hawke's Bay.

Visitors in search of the esoteric might want to stray well off the beaten track along State Hwy 52, which loops east of State Hwy 2 in southern Hawke's Bay. Some 6km south of the coastal hamlet of Porangahau, a sign marks the hill known as **Taumatawhakatangihangakoauauotamateaturipukakapik imaungahoonukapkaiwhenuakitanatahu**, which, unsurprisingly, rates as the world's longest place name. The local Ngati Kere celebrate their ancestor and warrior chief, Tamatea Pokai Whenua, who had to fight the Ngati Hine people to pass through the area. Tamatea's brother was killed, and in grief Tamatea would play a daily lament on his *koauau* (flute), hence the rough translation "the hilltop where Tamatea with big knees, conqueror of mountains, eater of land, traveller over land and sea, played his *koauau* to his beloved". It is a lament still heard at *tangi* (funerals).

Cape Palliser

55km southeast of Wellington and 140km by road via Martinborough.

The bleak and windswept coast around **Cape Palliser** – the southernmost point on the North Island – has a rich Maori past. Many ancestors of the Ngati Hinewaka people are buried along this coast, making it a sacred place. The road to the cape passes the **Putangirua Pinnacles**, dozens of grey soft-rock spires and fluted cliffs up to 50m high, formed by wind and rain eroding the surrounding silt and gravel. The pinnacles can be reached along an easy streambed path (1hr return). Nearby, the slabs of rock known as **Nga ra o Kupe** (Kupe's Sails) are said to resemble sails straining in the stiff Cook Strait southerlies. Traces of twelfth-century stone walls along the coastal terraces around **Te Humenga Point** are some of the earliest Maori occupation sites recorded in New Zealand. At the cape itself, 250 steps climb up to **Cape Palliser lighthouse**, where the largest breeding colony of fur seals in the North Island lies right beside the road.

MAORI CULTURAL EXPERIENCES

Long Island Tours ⊤06/877 0977, ⓦwww.longislandtoursnz .com. Napier-based guided tours, ranging from half a day ($190) meeting artists, sampling wine and exploring the area, to full-day trips (from $400) focused on Maori heritage and including a *marae* visit.

Hawaiki 100 Main St, Greytown ⊤06/304 7223, ⓔarotahi@xtra .co.nz. Specialist boutique, 70km northeast of Wellington, selling authentic Maori and Polynesian art and *taonga* (treasures).

Matahiwi Marae ⊤06/870 0602, ⓔtommulligan@xtra

.co.nz. One of the oldest established Ngati Hawea *marae* in Hawke's Bay is at Haumoana, 17km south of Napier, near the mouth of the Tukituki River and surrounded by orchards and vines. The two-hour visit ($20) consists of *powhiri* (welcome), plus an explanation of *marae* life and protocols.

Matariki Wines ⊤06/879 6226, ⓦwww.matarikiwines.co.nz. Boutique winery on the outskirts of Hastings which takes its name from the Maori New Year. The owners work closely with the Hawke's Bay Matariki festival each June.

Taranaki

T he *rohe* of **Taranaki** – renowned for its rich farmlands
and superb gardens – forms a bulge on the North
Island's west coast, and stretches from Mokau in the
north to Waitotara in the south; the provincial capital, **New
Plymouth**, lies on the northern shore of the bulge.

The *rohe* is characterised by three distinct areas: the icy
summit of **Mount Taranaki** which, according to Maori legend, once stood at the centre of the North Island; the lower
hill country, supporting pastoral farming and commercial
forestry; and the coastal terraces to the north and south,
which boast some of the best surfing and windsurfing in the
country. Taranaki has a population of about 100,000, of
whom fifteen percent are Maori. **Iwi** include Ngati Tama,
Ngati Mutunga, Te Ati Awa, Ngati Maru, Taranaki, Nga
Ruahine, Ngati Ruanui and Nga Rauru, and they largely
trace their *whakapapa* back to the Great Migratory canoes of
Aotea and Kurahaupo.

Taranaki already had a well-established oral narrative of
tribal warfare before it became central to the outbreak of the
main phase of the **New Zealand Wars** in the early 1860s.
Over the last two decades, successive governments have established a process to settle historical grievances relating to land
confiscation, and most Taranaki *iwi* are at various stages of
negotiation. The Ngati Mutunga and Te Ati Awa have agreements with the government for financial redress worth $14.5
million and $34 million respectively, while the Nga Rauru
have already settled for $31 million. The discovery of large

deposits of natural gas off the Taranaki coast in the early 1970s diverted local economic attention from milk and cheese towards petrochemical industries. However gas supplies are dwindling, and question marks surround the future of the industry. There's more regional **information** on Ⓦwww .taranakinz.org.

Puke Ariki

1 Ariki St, New Plymouth Ⓦwww.pukeariki.com. Mon, Tues, Thurs, Fri 9am–6pm; Weds 9am–9pm; Sat & Sun 9am–5pm. Admission free.

Taranaki's provincial museum, library and information centre is known as **Puke Ariki** – literally "Hill of Chiefs" – recalling the nearby *pa* site beside which the modern town of New Plymouth was founded. Along with displays on natural history and settler life there's an extensive Maori collection, **Te Takapou Whariki o Taranaki Gallery** (The Sacred Woven Mat of Taranaki). Here, the stories are told not by historians and social scientists but, refreshingly, by the *tangata whenua* (the people of the land) themselves who help interpret the *taonga* (treasures) on show. Highlights include the anchor stone from the Tokomaru *waka*, which brought Taranaki Maori to New Zealand, and volcanic rock carvings and wood carvings of a style unique to Taranaki, with three-dimensional figures (unlike many Maori carvings which are reliefs on a flat background).

Parihaka

Mid Parihaka Rd, just off State Hwy 45, 40km southwest of New Plymouth. *Marae* visits by appointment, call ☎06/763 8708.

A small Taranaki settlement located halfway between Mount Taranaki and the Tasman Sea, **Parihaka** village is of immense historical and cultural significance as the genesis of the New Zealand Wars. With trouble brewing, caused by hastily arranged land purchases and a government intent on colonising the area, 1500 militia and members of the Armed Constabulary invaded the settlement on November 5, 1881. The Maori inhabitants at the time were led by Te Whiti O Rongomai (of Taranaki and Te Ati Awa descent) and Tohu Kakahi (of Taranaki and Ngati Ruanui descent), both of whom advocated non-violence, drawing on their Maori and Christian teachings. As surveyors attempted to mark out the proposed new territory, Maori, spurred on by Te Whiti and Tohu, urged peaceful protest by removing marker pegs and erecting fences across lands and roads. More than two thousand Maori sat quietly on the *marae* as a group of singing children greeted the army. The Riot Act was read and one hour later Te Whiti and Tohu were arrested and led away. The village itself was demolished in the following months, while crops were destroyed and livestock killed. The suffering caused by the confiscation of tribal lands, and the imprisonment of Parihaka men (some were held for up to eighteen years, without trial), remains a painful legacy for the community.

Mount Taranaki and Egmont National Park

Access from North Egmont visitor centre, 27km south of New Plymouth, or Dawson Falls visitor centre, 20km west of Stratford. Both open daily 8am–4.30pm. For information follow the "National Parks" link at Ⓦ www.doc.govt.nz.

Iconic **Mount Taranaki** (2518m) is linked by legend to the mountains of the central North Island – Ruapehu, Ngauruhoe and Tongariro. It is said that Taranaki made his affections known to another mountain, Pihanga, but lost the fight for her heart to Tongariro, which stands proudly in the heart of the central North Island. Losing the battle, Taranaki carved out the bed of the Whanganui River on a tragic flight to the coast, resurfacing at its current location. Mount Taranaki is the centrepiece of **Egmont National Park**, which at 33,500 hectares is New Zealand's third-smallest national park, yet it attracts over 200,000 visitors a year. Visitors come to amble gently through the native bush to beautiful waterfalls such as **Dawson Falls** or to walk through the Goblin Forest to **Wilkies Pools** – a series of plunge pools formed by the scouring action of waterborne sand and gravel.

Tawhiti Museum

401 Ohangai Rd, 4km east of Hawera, 80km south of New Plymouth Ⓦ www.yellow.co.nz/site/tawhitimuseum. Christmas–Jan daily, otherwise Fri–Mon 10am–4pm, Sun only June, July & August. Admission $8.

Tawhiti Museum, just outside the small country town of Hawera, features a unique series of sixty-odd life-sized figurines modelled on local people by owner, creator and visionary Nigel Ogle. The social and technological heritage of both Maori and Pakeha is explored through the extensive use of photographs, models and dioramas, some of the most impressive being representations of *pa* sites. Note the model of the virtually impregnable Turuturumokai *pa*, and the changes to fortifications demanded by the advent of musket warfare.

MAORI CULTURAL EXPERIENCES

Art Maori Limited Richmond Shopping Centre, 4 Egmont St, New Plymouth ☎ 06/769 9056, Ⓦ www.artmaori.co.nz. Traditional and contemporary Maori arts, including carving and *ta moko* (tattooing), and works by owners Julie and Rangi Kipa.

Kaitiaki Adventures ☎ 021/461 110, Ⓦ www.damdrop.com. Local Maori *kaitiaki* (guardians) of the Waingongoro River, in the shadow of Mount Taranaki, offer the thrill of "dam dropping", or water sledging down the face of a small dam. It costs $50 for the first dam drop and $20 for each subsequent go, or try the full river run ($80).

Mount Taranaki Adventures ☎ 06/764 6585, Ⓦ www.mtt .org.nz. Cultural and adventure tour (3–4hr, $120, though less for groups) that explores Maori tracks and secret locations on Mount Taranaki, finishing with a 14-kilometre downhill cycle trip through bush and farmland on the return to Kaponga.

Taranaki Tours ☎ 0800/886 877, Ⓦ www.taranakitours.com. Small-group tours led by a knowledgeable Maori guide, who shares Taranaki legends, history and culture. Mountain shuttle $40, volcano tour $120, full-day adventure package $250.

Whanganui and Manawatu

Two *rohe* – Whanganui and Manawatu – spread across a back-country area of the western North Island that is still relatively under-visited by tourists and New Zealanders. The **Whanganui** *rohe* follows its eponymous river from Mount Tongariro through the spectacular Whanganui National Park to the provincial capital, Wanganui city, and thence to the coast of the Tasman Sea. The **Manawatu** *rohe* starts at Mangaweka in the north and goes as far south as Foxton, cutting back east through the provincial capital of Palmerston North to the Manawatu Gorge. The **iwi** of the *rohe* include Ngati Haua, Te Ati Hau, Ngati Raukawa, Ngati Apa, Rangitane and Muaupoko.

Centrepiece of the region is the **Whanganui River**, at 291km the longest navigable river in Aotearoa. More than a mere landmark, it is regarded as the soul of Maori from the area, as it has been for forty generations. They have relied upon it for sustenance, transport, economic development and spiritual well-being. In Maori mythology the river was formed after a battle between Mount Tongariro and Mount Taranaki for the affections of Mount Pihanga. Taranaki lost and in retreat cut a path to the Tasman that today is the Whanganui River. It is Taranaki's tears, they say, that filled the river. Though Kupe, the legendary Polynesian discoverer of Aotearoa, is said to have found the Whanganui River, it is Tamatea, captain of the Takitimu *waka*, who is credited with the first full exploration. The descendants of the Aotea *waka* subsequently established several fortified villages at defensible riverside sites. Europeans first arrived close to the modern city of **Wanganui** in 1831 and, by 1840, the New Zealand Company was staking claim to the area having already outgrown its possessions around Wellington. By 1860, Wanganui had a population of around two thousand, and it has continued to grow (whilst retaining the anglicised version of the river name for its name).

The river provided an important means of communication and transportation between local villages, and gained in importance as returning soldiers from World War I began breaking in new farms along the banks of the riverbanks. The highly scenic river also soon proved a popular tourist destination – the "Rhine of the South Pacific" – a role it still plays today as part of the **Whanganui National Park**. In addition to jetboat rides, today's visitors are also offered adventure tours and *marae* stays by local Maori operators. For further **information** try ⓦ www.whanganuiriver.co.nz, ⓦ www.destinationwanganui .com and ⓦ www.manawatunz.co.nz.

Whanganui Regional Museum

Watt St, Wanganui ⓦ www.wanganui-museum.org.nz. Daily 10am–4.30pm. Admission $5.

The **Whanganui Regional Museum** contains an outstanding collection of Maori artefacts, tools, weapons, garments, ornaments, musical instruments and three impressive canoes, all displayed in Te Ati Haunui-a-Paparangi, the central court that is shaped like a traditional meeting house. Hung around the collection and in smaller galleries off the main area are works by Bohemian immigrant, Gottfried Lindauer, who came to New Zealand in 1873 and spent his later years painting portraits of high-born Maori. Other exhibits include a reconstruction of an early street in the Pakeha settlement, and displays on New

Zealand natural history, including a large number of skeletons of *moa*, the large flightless bird hunted to extinction by early Maori settlers.

Moutoa Gardens

Somme Parade, Wanganui.

Moutoa Gardens is an innocuous-looking patch of grass in the centre of Wanganui that has become symbolic of Maori attempts to redress past wrongs. Traditionally, Maori lived at Moutoa during the fishing season until it was co-opted by Pakeha settlers. Later, Maori signed the document agreeing to the "sale" of Wanganui, an issue revisited on Waitangi Day 1995 when simmering old grievances and one or two more recent ones reached boiling point. A long Maori occupation ended peacefully when the High Court threw out the Maori claim on the land, but the events created much bitterness on both sides, neither of which particularly distinguished itself during the occupation. A more creative atmosphere now prevails with the government, city council and local *iwi* sharing management of the gardens.

Whanganui National Park

Most facilities and services are found in Taumarunui and Wanganui (regular bus services to both), which each have DOC offices. Various companies run shuttles to the trailheads and canoe drop-offs.

The Whanganui River falls within the **Whanganui National Park**, and the best way to explore is on a river-trip – by canoe, kayak or jetboat – with one of the region's specialist operators (see listings below). With them you'll learn something of the river's unique importance to Maori, who may have settled the valley from 1100 AD. Every bend of the river had a *kaitiaki* (guardian), which controlled the *mauri* (life force) of that place. The *mana* (prestige) of a settlement depended upon the way in which food supplies and living areas were looked after for the benefit of the tribe and visitors. Elaborate weirs were erected along river channels where eels and lamprey were known to converge, while sheltered terraces were cultivated and a series of fortified villages erected on strategic heights.

The slow and winding **Whanganui River Road** runs beside the river for much of its lower reaches, providing access to the tiny community of Hiruharama, and Pipiriki, departure point for jetboat trips upriver to the so-called **Bridge to Nowhere** in the remote Mangapurua Valley. Built in 1936 to provide access to a rural pioneer settlement, which was subsequently abandoned, the bridge is now the only reminder as regenerating bush has long since covered the track.

Pipiriki is also the pull-out point for the kayak or **canoe trips**, which usually start several days' upstream at Taumarunui or Whakahoro. There are also a variety of walks for the more adventurous, prime amongst them the **Matemateonga Track** (3–4 days one way), which follows an old Maori trail and settlers' dray road deep into the park.

Tieke Marae

21km upstream from Pipiriki, river access only.

The riverside setting of **Tieke Marae** is an old *pa* site later used as a location for a DOC hut. The hut was later re-occupied by local Maori for whom it has become a kind of informal *marae* that welcomes river users on a first-come-first-served basis. The *marae* isn't always occupied, but if residents are around you're welcomed on to the site with traditional protocols: *powhiri* (welcome), *hongi* (greeting by pressing noses) and *whaikorero* (the exchange of oratory). You'll be expected to reply (perhaps saying something of your lineage or where you're from), perhaps perform a song, and lay a monetary gift (*koha*) on the ground after speaking. Once the formalities are over, everyone then proceeds to the dining room, where the meal is usually cooked and eaten together.

TIEKE MARAE

Hiruharama

Whanganui River Rd, 10km south of Pipiriki.

Hiruharama (Maori for Jerusalem) – a picturesque village clinging tightly to its historical past – was originally a tribal village and Catholic mission but is now best known for the commune which briefly flourished here in the early 1970s. **James K. Baxter**, one of New Zealand's most (in)famous poets, attracted upwards of two hundred of his followers to the area. A devout Roman Catholic convert, but also firm believer in free love in his search for a "New Jerusalem", he became father to a flock of his own, the *nga moki* (fatherless ones), who soon dispersed after his death in 1972. The main commune house is situated high on a hill, and Baxter is buried just below the house. Two remaining Sisters of Compassion still live here, regarded as *kaitiaiki* (guardians) of the **church** (1892), which features a Maori-designed and carved altar. Also in the church

Ratana

Ratana Pa, 20km southeast of Wanganui, is the birthplace of a religious movement called Ratana, established by Maori prophet **Tahupotiki Wiremu Ratana** (1873–1939). Each January thousands of people descend on the tiny village to join in its annual festivities, including the country's political leaders anxious to win over the support of the religion's 60,000-plus followers. Indeed, the Ratana movement plays a significant part in New Zealand politics, with many Maori Members of Parliament being endorsed by Ratana leaders. The Ratana community was established during the 1920s as people came from all over the country to benefit from the prophet's ability to heal the sick – the walls around the church he built are covered with the walking sticks of those it is claimed were healed. The *marae*, too, is unlike any other in the country, its meeting house adorned with paintings of the seven ancestral *waka*, as well as representations of Abel Tasman's galleon *Heemskirk* and Cook's ship *Endeavour*.

HIRUHARAMA

is a photograph of Mother Mary Joseph Aubert (1835–1926), who established the first community of sisters in 1892, and a portrait of Baxter, looking suitably messianic.

Te Ahu-a-Turanga
Manawatu Gorge, 15km northeast of Palmerston North.

The **Manawatu Gorge** had a special significance for early Maori, as it was the only low-level route between the Ruahine and Tararua ranges, allowing passage between the western and eastern portions of the North Island. They named the gorge Te Apiti ("the narrow passage") and the river Te Au-Rere-a-Te-Tonga ("the rushing current of the south"), while the large reddish-coloured rock that stands in the Manawatu River near the centre of the gorge was named **Te Ahu-a-Turanga** – "the sacred place of Turanga", ancient ancestor of the Rangitane people of the Manawatu. The rock was considered the guardian spirit of the gorge, a place where Maori travelling by canoe would recite *karakia* (prayers) to ensure their safety. Legend has it that the rock always remains above water even when the river experiences its highest floods. Its red colour is said to change in intensity if a prominent member of the local Rangitane tribe dies or if blood is shed.

MAORI CULTURAL EXPERIENCES

Aorangi Experiences ☎ 06/388 1444, Ⓦ www.hikoitreks.co.nz. Aorangi-led 7hr "cultural hikes" ($129) in the Ruahine ranges near Taihape, 110km north of Palmerston North, learning about the flora and fauna and its significance to Maori.
John Bevan Ford Art Gallery ☎ 06/326 8187, Ⓦ www.fordart.co.nz. Call in advance before visiting the Ashhurst studio (15km east of Palmerston North) of this internationally renowned Maori artist whose works – particularly large wooden carvings – grace galleries as far afield as Beijing, London and Amsterdam.

Koriniti Marae ☎ 021/365 176, ⓦ www.whanganuiriver.co.nz /korinitimarae.html. Whanganui River *marae* open to groups, who are welcomed with a *powhiri*, supplied with meals (including a *hangi*), entertained with Maori songs and dance, and provided with simple accommodation, for $85 a day.

Waka Tours ☎ 06/385 4811, ⓦ www.wakatours.net. Three-day guided canoe tour (Oct–April, $560) with local Maori who are passionate about the Whanganui River and its history. You'll take in many of the historical sites, including an overnight stay on a *marae*.

Whanganui River Guides ☎ 07/896 6726, ⓦ www.whanganuiriverguides. co.nz. One-day ($150) and multi-day ($200 per day) canoe trips with Maori guides who give a real sense of what it must have been like to live along the river.

Te Upoko o Te Ika

T he *rohe* of **Te Upoko o Te Ika** occupies the southern tip of the North Island, taking in the western Kapiti and eastern Wairarapa coasts, and stretching southwards as far as Wellington. Te Upoko o Te Ika means "the head of the fish", a reference to the fish hooked by Maori demigod Maui when he pulled the North Island from the sea. The **iwi** of the *rohe* include Te Ati Awa and Ngati Toa.

The *rohe* is centred on the nation's capital city, **Wellington**, whose harbour was first sighted by Polynesian explorer Kupe around the tenth century. However, it is known by Maori as Te Whanganui a Tara – "the great harbour of Tara" – after Whatonga of Hawke's Bay, who sent his son Tara to inspect the lower North Island. Evidence of early Maori settlement and cultivation can be found at sites all round the Wellington peninsula. It was not until 1840 that the first wave of European settlers arrived, not long after the New Zealand Company had purchased a large tract of land around the harbour. The first settlement, known as Britannia, was established on the north-eastern beaches at Petone; shortly after, the Hutt River flood-ed, forcing the settlers to move around the harbour to a more sheltered site. During the nineteenth century Wellington (named by the British after the Duke of Wellington, soldier, statesman and prime minister) flourished as a hub of coastal shipping and trade, and in 1865 superseded Auckland as capital of New Zealand, largely because of its central location and fine harbour. For city and regional **information** consult Ⓦ www.wellingtonnz.com.

Parliament Buildings

Molesworth St, Wellington Ⓦ www.parliament.govt.nz. Free 1hr tours depart regularly from the ground floor foyer of Parliament House, Mon–Fri 10am–4pm, Sat 10am–3pm, Sun noon–3pm.

The heart of New Zealand's government lies in the **Parliament Buildings**, a trio of structures including the Victorian Gothic Parliamentary Library and the modernist **Beehive**, a seven-stepped truncated cone which houses the cabinet and the offices of its ministers. Between these stands the Neoclassical **Parliament House**, whose highlight is the extremely decorative **Maori Affairs Select Committee Room** with its specially commissioned carvings and *tukutuku* (woven panels) from all the major tribal groups in the land. It is set aside for *nga take Maori* (Maori affairs). If Parliament isn't sitting, you are led through the Debating Chamber, while if the house is in session you are free to wander into the public gallery to observe proceedings after the tour.

Maori in Parliament

Maori reached a low ebb towards the end of the nineteenth century with their population decreasing and the language on the wane. However, as resistance to European diseases grew, numbers started to rise, accompanied by a new confidence buoyed by the rise of Maori parliamentary leadership in the early 1900s. **Apirana Ngata**, **Maui Pomare** and **Te Rangi Hiroa (Peter Buck)** were all products of Te Aute College, an Anglican school for Maori. All were committed to working within government, convinced that the survival of *Maoritanga* depended on shedding those aspects of the traditional lifestyle that impeded their acceptance of the modern world. Maori have subsequently been represented in Parliament both through dedicated **Maori seats** (originally four and now seven out of a total of 120), and by taking general seats. In 1996 the country threw out the old Westminster-style Parliament and voted in its first government under the Mixed Member Proportional system, which allowed for greater representation of minor parties. A new Maori spirit entered Parliament, with far more Maori MPs than ever before (accounting for almost seventeen percent of MPs), whose maiden speeches are received with a *waiata* (song) from their *whanau* (extended family) in the public gallery.

Archives New Zealand

10 Mulgrave St, Wellington ⓦ www.archives.govt.nz. Mon–Fri 9am–5pm, Sat 9am–1pm. Admission free.

The bulk of the country's most sacred documents are on display in the **Constitution Room**, a dimly lit vault at Archives New Zealand. The prize exhibit is the original Maori-language Treaty of Waitangi, lost until 1908 and still exhibiting signs of water and rat damage. Other archives highlight important milestones on the country's road to independent nationhood, notably Maori petitions dating back to 1909, which complain of broken treaty promises, and a facsimile of the 1893 petition for women's suffrage. Outside the Constitution Room is a small container of water, to help Maori neutralise *tapu* (ill-effects caused by a taboo action) after viewing the treaty. Mounted on a wall nearby is an enlarged copy of the treaty and a map, showing who signed where; the great Maori chief Te Rauparaha signed it twice, in different locations, each time receiving muskets and blankets.

Te Papa – the Museum of New Zealand

Cable St, Wellington Ⓦ www.tepapa.govt.nz. Daily 10am–6pm, until 9pm on Thurs. Admission free, daily guided tours $10.

Te Papa – the Museum of New Zealand – is Wellington's star attraction, a purpose-built five-storey building right on the waterfront, which opened in 1998. The hub is on Level 2, where there are all manner of interactive experiences, including the chance to watch Mount Ruapehu erupt on screen and hear the Maori explanation of the causes of such activity. Then step up to Level 4 for the excellent Maori section, which incorporates a thought-provoking display on the Treaty of Waitangi dominated by a giant glass image of this formative document. There's also an active *marae* with a modern meeting house painted in a rainbow of pastel colours and protected by a sacred boulder of *pounamu* (greenstone); you are not allowed to enter the meeting house unless invited. Colonial history is covered in the "Passports" section, while the "Mana Whenua" exhibit has a great collection of *taonga* (treasures) supplemented by a rotating programme of displays by individual *iwi*: the Whanganui exhibition runs until May 2006.

Pataka Museum

Cnr Norrie and Parumoana streets, Porirua, 20km north of Wellington Ⓦ www.pataka.org.nz. Mon–Sat 10am–4.30pm, Sun 11am–4.30pm. Admission free.

Pataka is a combined museum, art gallery and library set up to promote contemporary Maori, Pacific Island and New Zealand arts and crafts. Temporary exhibitions focus on particular aspects of traditional Maori craft – from cloak-weaving to stone-carving – while there's also a strong emphasis on contemporary art and design, from jewellery to ceramics. The art of other indigenous peoples is often presented, too, with the pretty garden-café the place to unwind after a visit.

Kapiti Island

5km off the west coast of the southern North Island near Paraparaumu, 45km north of Wellington. Daily boat service from Paraparaumu Beach with Kapiti Tours ($35 return, Ⓦ www.kapititours.co.nz), and guided visits with Kapiti Island Alive, see listing below.

Kapiti Island is one of the few easily accessible island nature reserves in New Zealand. This 10km-long by 2km-wide summit of a submerged mountain range is cloaked in regenerating bush, home to birdlife that has become rare or extinct on the mainland – *kaka* (bush parrots), *weka*, *kakariki* (parakeets), bush canaries, *tui*, bellbirds, fantails, wood pigeons, robins and a handful of the two hundred *takahe* that exist in the world. The birdlife is at its most active in late January and February but you can explore the island at any time on three walking tracks, two of them linking up to the island's summit (521m), which gives spectacular views. The North Track (2–3hr) follows the coast to the island's northern end, leading to a lagoon thronged with waterfowl.

In 1822, warrior chief Te Rauparaha captured the island from its first known Maori inhabitants and, with his people the Ngati Toa, used it as a base until his death in 1849. It's thought that he may be buried somewhere on the island, but the site of his grave is unknown. For this, and other reasons, the island is considered extremely spiritual to Maori, and was designated a reserve in 1897. In addition, the exceptionally clear waters between Kapiti Island and the coast are a marine reserve that's home to orange and yellow sponges and luxuriant seaweed beds feeding *kina* (sea urchins) and *paua* (native abalone).

KAPITI ISLAND

Rangiatea Church

Te Rauparaha St, 2.5km off State Hwy 1, Otaki, 65km north of Wellington Ⓦhttp://rangiatea.natlib.govt.nz.

What was once recognised as the finest of all Maori churches burned down in 1995, but Ngati Toa, who built the original in around 1850, have recently opened a faithful replica of **Rangiatea Church**. The original church was commissioned by Ngati Toa chief Te Rauparaha, who was buried in the cemetery outside (under two Norfolk pines). Legend has it that the burial didn't accord with his chiefly status and Ngati Toa subsequently reinterred him on Kapiti Island (see above) with due pomp. More certain is the craftsmanship and dedication that has gone into re-creating the new church's superb carved interior.

MAORI CULTURAL EXPERIENCES

Kapiti Island Alive & Kapiti Nature Lodge ☎06/362 6606, Ⓦwww.kapitiislandalive.co.nz. Visit the Maori-owned northern tip of Kapiti Island for a day's walking and bird-spotting ($110), or stay overnight in the comfortable lodge ($220) with the opportunity to go looking for Little Spotted Kiwi.

Kura Contemporary Ethnic Art 19 Allen St, Wellington ☎04/802 4934, Ⓦwww.kuragallery.co.nz. The Wellington branch of this established Auckland gallery exhibits quality contemporary New Zealand art works.

Maori Treasures ☎04/939 9630. Arts and crafts centre in Lower Hutt, Wellington, that's the base of master carver Rangi Hetet and his wife, the weaver Erenora Puketapu-Hetet. A three-hour visit ($85) includes a chance to watch artists at work and then try your hand at creating something from bone, stone, wood or flax. The full-day tour ($210) adds in hotel pick-up, a guided tour of Te Papa and a whole lot more.

Te Tau Ihu

T he *rohe* of **Te Tau Ihu** covers the northern tip of the South Island embracing the Nelson-Marlborough Sounds region and Golden Bay. The name derives from the phrase Te Tau Ihu o Te Waka a Maui, which means "the prow of the canoe of Maui" (ie, the South Island), from which Maui the demigod fished up the North Island. The **iwi** of the *rohe* include Ngati Tama, Te Ati Awa, Rangitane, Ngati Toa, Ngati Rarua, Ngati Apa, Ngati Koata and Ngati Kuia.

Polynesian voyagers first arrived in the area around eight hundred years ago aboard the Uruao *waka*. The banks of the Waimea River, and the sites of the modern towns of Motueka,

Getting creative

With its profusion of craftspeople and vibrant arts scene, Te Tau Ihu is an ideal place to learn something about Maori ways. The easiest way to access what's on offer is through **Creative Tourism** (Ⓦ www.creativetourism.co.nz), which co-ordinates regional Maori cultural workshops. In Nelson, you can visit the *marae* of the local Whakatu *iwi* ($100), devote a few hours to learning the *haka* ($90), spend the day learning Maori ways of gathering seafood ($100), or combine one of these with a *hangi* and overnight stay on the *marae* ($650). Alternatively head out to the hills nearby to experience *harakeke* weaving ($90), where, under the experienced eye of Arohanui Ropata, you should end the session with some flax flowers and small baskets.

Riwaka, Mapua and Parpara, have long histories with evidence of early gardens. The produce was supplemented by abundant seafood and bird life. Being at the geographic centre of Aotearoa, Te Tau Ihu was a trading hotspot, with North Island Maori often resting here before continuing down the West Coast to trade for *pounamu* (greenstone). Other Maori traders journeyed to the Maitahi Valley to gain access to the *pakohe*, the stone most commonly used for making tools.

Te Tau Ihu Maori were the first to come into contact with Europeans when, in 1642, Dutchman **Abel Tasman** sailed into what is now known as Golden Bay. Before Tasman had a chance to land, Maori ambushed one of his longboats and four sailors were killed. Tasman slunk off and Aotearoa was left in peace for over a century until English navigator, **Captain James Cook**, arrived in 1769 (and again in 1773 and 1777). His visits were more peaceful, and he particularly liked the Marlborough Sounds, spending a total of three months in Ship Cove in the Queen Charlotte Sound, taking on fresh water and supplies.

From **Picton**, the ferry port for the Cook Strait crossing from Wellington, cruises and kayak trips leave for the **Marlborough Sounds**, and it's also the departure point for hikers on the Queen Charlotte Track; while just to the south **Blenheim** is surrounded by the famed Marlborough wine country. To the west, **Nelson** was one of the first cities to be established in colonial times, and remains the largest in the northern South Island. It is used as a base for forays north to the **Abel Tasman National Park**, with its wonderful coastal walking and kayaking, and beyond to the wilderness of **Farewell Spit**. For regional **information** visit Ⓦwww.DestinationMarlborough.com, Ⓦwww.nelsonnz.com and Ⓦwww.abeltasmangreenrush.co.nz.

Karaka Point Pa

Port Underwood Rd, 8km northeast of Picton. Unrestricted access.

The **Karaka Point Pa** was originally called Te Rae o Te

Karaka, after Ngati Mamoe chief Te Karaka who settled here in the early 1700s. The *pa* was stormed by Ngai Tahu in around 1720 and Te Karaka was killed, leaving the survivors to inter-marry with Ngai Tahu. In the 1820s, the Te Ati Awa tribe attacked the *pa* with muskets. The defenders were routed and massacred and the *pa* was burned to the ground. Today, you can explore the grassy earthworks that constitute the remains of the *pa* on a short walk, which provides great views across Queen Charlotte Sound.

The Suter

208 Bridge St, Nelson ⓦ www.thesuter.org.nz. Daily 10.30am–4.30pm. Admission $3.

One of the finest public art museums in the South Island, **The Suter** is also known as Te Aratoi o Whakatu – "the art path-way of the Whakatu" *hapu* (sub-tribe). Particular significance is given to a famous 1909 portrait by Gottfried Lindauer of Huria Matenga, a Maori woman, who with her husband and friends saved many lives from the wreck of the American ship *Delaware* in 1863. Her status is indicated by *moko* (traditional tattoos), feathers, bone, greenstone jewellery and the ceremonial club she holds; in the background is the foundering vessel. The gallery constantly changes its displays, but usually includes oils by "Toss" Woollaston, a founder of the modernist movement in New Zealand art.

Abel Tasman National Park

State Hwy 60, 50km north of Nelson (regular bus service). Kayaks and cruises available from Marahau and Kaiteriteri Beach, north of Motueka, see listings below.

For over five hundred years, Maori lived (at least for part of the year) along the coast of what is now the **Abel Tasman National Park**, fishing, gathering *kai moana* (seafood), and growing *kumara*. It was here, in 1642, that Abel Tasman had his fateful brush with local Maori in what he called "Murderers'

Bay", though it wasn't until the mid-nineteenth century that European settlement began in earnest. The settlers chopped, quarried, burned and cleared until nothing was left but gorse and bracken, though happily few signs of their invasion remain today. The national park was established in 1942 and the vegetation has vigorously regenerated over the years. In summer, visitors flock here to walk the easy two-day **Coastal Track**, or kayak along the same stretch of coastline.

Waikoropupu Springs

Just off State Hwy 60, 4km north of Takaka. Unrestricted access.

Waikoropupu Springs, long known by their anglicised moniker of "Pupu Springs", are New Zealand's largest freshwater springs, pumping out some 15 cubic metres per second at 12°C. The crystal clear water emanates from sixteen vents, two large examples filling the main pool and a third enlivening the "Dancing Sands" where the sands are agitated by the surging water. The colourful aquatic plant life can be seen by means of a large reverse periscope on one of the boardwalks.

To Maori, the springs are both *taonga* (treasure) and *waahi tapu* (a sacred place) providing water for healing as well as being a place of ceremony for births and deaths. People are asked to respect this sanctity and not to swim or dive in the springs themselves; however, drift dives down certain streams are permitted.

Kahurangi National Park

Northwestern corner of the South Island. Easiest access is from Takaka (useful visitor centre) and Karamea. In summer, regular buses run to the start of the Heaphy Track.

Kahurangi ("treasured possession") is New Zealand's second largest national park; 40,000 square kilometres of barely tracked wilderness, wild rivers, deep caves, high plateaus, alpine herb fields and coastal forests. The park enfolds the western side of the Wakamarama Range, which are among the wettest mountains in the country and include the peaks of Mount Owen and

Mount Arthur. Maori seeking *pounamu* (greenstone) along the West Coast cut the first tracks across Kahurangi, and there are now over 500km of trails including the popular 82-kilometre, five-day, **Heaphy Track** (one of New Zealand's Great Walks). Shorter day-walks are possible from the fringes of the park and local shuttle-buses provide trailhead transport.

Farewell Spit

State Hwy 60, 140km north of Nelson. Visitor centre 26km north of Collingwood open Sept–June daily 9am–5pm, closed July & Aug. Farewell Spit Safari costs $70 Ⓦ www.farewell-spit.co.nz.

Effectively an overgrown sand bar (the world's longest), **Farewell Spit** forms a graceful 25-kilometre curve at the northern tip of the South Island. Evidence from middens indicate that it was inhabited for seven hundred years by Maori, who know it as Onetahua ("heaped up sand"). In 1846, explorer Charles Heaphy reported seeing *waka* (Maori canoes) heading to the ocean beach and down the West Coast. You can see evidence of Maori habitation at the road-accessible **Puponga Farm Park**, and can walk on the first couple of kilometres of sand, but to get right out in the spit to the abandoned lighthouse station and gannet colony you'll need to join the 4WD Farewell Spit Safari, complete with bright commentary peppered with local lore.

MAORI CULTURAL EXPERIENCES

Abel Tasman Adventures

☏ 03/527 8032,
Ⓦ www.abeltasmankayaks.co.nz. Kayak tours ($75 for half a day, plus assorted longer trips) giving a Maori perspective on the Abel Tasman National Park coast and the customary practices of its people.

Abel Tasman Waka Tours

☏ 03/527 8160,
Ⓦ www.wakatours.co.nz. Paddle along the shores in a traditionally carved *waka*. Guides talk about Maori culture and local history, leaving plenty of time to swim and relax. Half-day tour $130.

Myths & Legends Eco Tours
☎ 03/573 6901, ⓦ www.eco-tours.co.nz. Sixth-generation Kiwi, Pete Beech, and his Maori wife, Takutai, take you out into the Marlborough Sounds on an eco-oriented wildlife and cultural cruise, highlighting fascinating stories handed down through their Maori and Pakeha families. Half day $150, full day $200, overnight cruises by arrangement.

Tohu Wines Limited ☎ 04/566 3446, ⓦ www.tohuwines.co.nz. Export-quality wines produced by a partnership of Blenheim Maori groups. There are currently no cellar door sales or tastings, though you can sample the wines – Chardonnay, Sauvignon Blanc and Pinot Noir – at restaurants like *The Boatshed* and *Fish Bizarre* in Nelson, *Bragato's Wine Bar* in Blenheim and *Finz* of South Bay in Kaikoura.

Te Waipounamu

Te Waipounamu is the largest *rohe*, covering eighty percent of the South Island – in fact everything south of the line from Kaikoura in the east to Karamea on the West Coast, including Stewart Island (Rakiura). The predominant **iwi** of the *rohe* is Ngai Tahu, which has tribal authority over an area five times larger than any other *iwi* and, with around 40,000 members, is the third largest in the country.

As early as 1800 Ngai Tahu were living in established settlements and travelling widely to trade or seek *pounamu* – the *rohe*

Making the most of the windfall

Since 1986, *iwi* have been able to claim restitution for wrongs done against them dating back to the signing of the Treaty of Waitangi in 1840. The process continues today through the Waitangi Tribunal, but several *iwi* have already settled their claims, including Ngai Tahu who, in 1998, accepted a sum of $170 million. Tribal leaders have managed the fund well, almost doubling their assets since then and establishing a sound economic base for Ngai Tahu descendants. Not only is Ngai Tahu one of the South Island's biggest landlords, it has become a key player in the fishing and tourism industries, taking full control of Queenstown's iconic Shotover Jet operation and planning a controversial cable-car system to speed access from Queenstown to Milford Sound. But it isn't just about making money. Each year millions are distributed for health, education and social and cultural development through their own development corporation.

name, Te Waipounamu, translates as "the place of greenstone". The tribe was quick to grasp the economic opportunities presented by the arrival of British settlers from 1839, who initially relied on Maori coastal trading – Ngai Tahu even traded potatoes, pigs, flax and vegetables as far as Sydney. In 1844, the British government made a series of ten major land purchases comprising much of the South Island. They drove a hard bargain, sometimes accompanied by threats, but ceded the right for Ngai Tahu to retain its *mahinga kai* – or food resources – and approximately a tenth of all land sold for their own use. The agreements weren't upheld but tribal representatives have subsequently settled the *iwi*'s longstanding historical grievances with the New Zealand government (see box).

For visitors, this part of the South Island is one of New Zealand's most exalted regions, encompassing the adventure capital of **Queenstown**, the gorgeous Fiordland scenery of **Milford Sound**, the cultured third city of **Christchurch** and, to the south, the Scottish-settled city of **Dunedin**, home to the country's oldest university. Those wanting to get off the beaten track should visit the lush and wild **West Coast**, while **Aoraki Mount Cook** and the snowy 3000-metre peaks of the **Southern Alps** are a draw for alpine climbers, hikers and skiers. Te Waipounamu also presents more opportunities to experience wildlife close-up than anywhere else in the country: whale-watching and dolphin swimming in **Kaikoura**; albatrosses and penguins on the **Otago Peninsula** near Dunedin; and predator-free bush that's alive with native birds on **Ulva Island**, just off Stewart Island. There's *iwi* **information** on Ⓦwww.ngaitahu .iwi.nz, while useful regional sites include Ⓦwww.queenstown-nz.co.nz, Ⓦwww.christchurchnz.net, Ⓦwww.dunedinnz.com, Ⓦwww.west-coast.co.nz and Ⓦwww.southlandnz.com.

Kura Tawhiti

State Hwy 73, 100km west of Christchurch. Open daylight hours. Admission free.

This swathe of rolling grassland peppered by clusters of house-sized grey limestone outcrops has long been known as Castle Hill, but now goes by the name **Kura Tawhiti** ("treasure from afar") in recognition of its spiritual significance to Ngai Tahu. One Ngai Tahu ancestor, Tane Tiki, is said to have come to the area in search of the now critically endangered flightless parrot, the *kakapo*. Its bright green feathers and soft skin were perfect for clothing for his daughter, Hine Mihi. Record of other visitors comes in the form of faint, 500-year-old charcoal drawings. Paths weave among the outcrops, and there are almost always rock climbers here, seemingly stuck to the sheer faces.

Okains Bay Maori and Colonial Museum

Okains Bay, Banks Peninsula, 40km southeast of Christchurch. Daily 10am–5pm. Admission $5.

A former cheese factory on the only road going into this tiny settlement now houses the **Okains Bay Maori and Colonial Museum**. Among the thought-provoking exhibits are a god stick dating back to 1400, a war canoe from 1867 and various weapons, as well as a valuable *hei tiki* (a pendant with a design based on the human form) recovered in England and brought back to Okains Bay. There is also a beautiful meeting house (it's *tapu* or sacred, although visitors are allowed to look around), with fine symbolic figures carved by master craftsman John Rua. Within the same compound, several outbuildings contain various exhibitions relating to European settlement, including a slab stable and cottage – simply constructed from large slabs of *totara* wood.

Aoraki Mount Cook

Central South Island, 200km west of Christchurch. Bus service to Aoraki Mount Cook Village from Twizel, Christchurch and Queenstown. For information follow National Parks link from Ⓦ www.doc.govt.nz.

New Zealand's highest mountain, **Aoraki Mount Cook** (3754m) goes by both its Maori name – meaning "cloud piercer" – and its more prosaic Pakeha equivalent honouring the great English navigator. Legend has it that Aoraki was a young boy sat with his brothers in the *waka* (canoe) that is the South Island. When stranded on a reef it tilted to one side and the south wind turned them all to stone, forming the Southern Alps (Ka Tiritiri o te Moana). The peak is the centrepiece of the largely icebound Aoraki Mount Cook National Park, and access to the mountainous terrain below the summit is from **Aoraki Mount Cook Village**, which grew up purely to cater for nineteenth-century tourists. Numerous walks fan out from the village ranging from easy strolls through native bush to stiff tramps up to the sub-alpine Mueller Hut with its great view of Aoraki.

Maori rock art sites

Several sites 15–20km northwest of Timaru
Ⓦ www.southisland.org.nz. Unrestricted access.

Around five hundred years ago, Maori *moa* hunters visited the South Canterbury and North Otago coastal plain, leaving a record of their sojourn on the walls and ceilings of open-sided limestone rock shelters. Several **Maori rock art sites** around Timaru contain more than three hundred faded charcoal and red ochre rock drawings depicting a variety of stylised human, bird and mythological figures and patterns. Drawings are often hard to make out, but the best examples are all marked on the *Pleasant Point Ward Map* from available from the Timaru visitor centre. The visitor centre can also organise access across private land to the sites.

Moeraki Boulders

State Hwy 1, 40km south of Oamaru. Unrestricted access along the beach or $2 in the honesty box by the café near the boulders.

Embedded in the beach and mostly covered at high tide, the spherical **Moeraki Boulders** are known to Maori as *Te Kaihinaki* ("food baskets"), apparently washed ashore from the wreck of a canoe whose occupants were seeking *pounamu*. The seaward reef near Shag Point to the south was the hull of the canoe, and just beyond it stands a prominent rock, the vessel's petrified navigator. Some of the Moeraki Boulders were *hinaki* (baskets), the more spherical were water-carrying gourds and the irregular-shaped rocks farther down the beach were *kumara* from the canoe's food store. The survivors among the crew, Nga Tamariki, Puketapu and Pakihiwi Tahi, were transformed at daybreak into hills overlooking the beach.

Despite appearances, the boulders did not fall from the sky, nor were they washed up by the sea, but rather lay deep in the mudstone cliffs behind the beach. As the sea eroded the cliffs, out fell the smooth boulders (some of which reach 2m in diameter), and their distinctive surface pattern was formed as further erosion exposed a network of veins. There used to be a large number of these boulders in the area, but the smaller ones have been pilfered over the years, leaving only those too heavy to shift.

MOERAKI BOULDERS

Takitimu Mountains

Off State Hwy 94, 15km southwest of Mossburn, 140km south of
Queenstown. Follow the "Tracks and Walks" link at
Ⓦ www.doc.govt.nz.

The **Takitimu Mountains** are named after the ancient Maori
migration *waka* Takitimu and is a place of cultural, spiritual and
historic value to Ngai Tahu. In their mythology, the captain of
the *waka*, Tamatea, named the mountains to commemorate the
wreck of his vessel in rough weather at the mouth of nearby Te
Wae Wae Bay. The *waka* was overtaken by three large waves,
which threw the vessel inland where the overturned hull
became the mountain range. Tramping access is via the
Aparima River Track on the eastern slopes, along which there
are several simple overnight huts.

MAORI CULTURAL EXPERIENCES

Dart Wilderness Adventures
Ⓣ 07/346 2823, Ⓦ www
.maoriculture.co.nz. Tales of the
region's Maori and European
settler traditions enhance the
jetboat ride up the Dart River,
through fabulous beech forest
and mountain scenery. Half-day
trip with barbecue $230 (until
end Sept 2006).

Haka Pa Queenstown
Ⓣ 03/442 1534, Ⓦ www
.maoriculture.net.nz. Rural site
where you're treated to the full
powhiri (greeting), dance and
hangi package for $89,
transport included.

**Ko Tane – The Maori
Experience** Ⓣ 03/359 6226,
Ⓦ www.kotane.co.nz. Excellent
cultural performance and *hangi*
(show $36, show & meal $82.50)
presented in a reconstructed
Maori village at the Willowbank
Wildlife Reserve in Christchurch.
It comes complete with a
traditional *powhiri* (greeting),
haka and *poi* dances before
retiring to the restaurant.

**Nga Hau E Wha National
Marae** Ⓣ 03/388 7685,
Ⓦ www.nationalmarae.co.nz.
The country's first urban
national *marae* (opened 1990)
was originally conceived as a
home for South Island Maori not
aligned with the dominant Ngai

Tahu *iwi*. Offers a cultural evening ($65) complete with formal welcome, *marae* tour, performance and *hangi*.

Maori Tours Kaikoura
☏ 03/319 5567, ⓦ www
.maoritours.co.nz. Kaikoura-based combination of educational forest walk, home visit and tour of *pa* sites (3–4hr, $85) with guides steeped in the culture of the local Ngati Kuri people.

The Bone Dude's Bone Carving Studio ☏ 03/379 7530, ⓦ www.thebonedude.co.nz. Small bone-carving studio in Christchurch, teaching skills and techniques along with the importance of creating a design that has meaning for you: direct copies of traditional pieces are strongly discouraged. Three-hour group sessions from $55 per person.

Ulva's Guided Walks
☏ 03/219 1216,
ⓦ www.ulva.co.nz. Stewart Island-based Ulva Amos runs leisurely walking tours (3hr, $85) around the island she was named after. Ulva Island – a short water-taxi ride across Paterson Inlet – is one of New Zealand's foremost open sanctuaries, and Ulva brings a knowledgeable Maori perspective to the island's native flora and fauna.

Whale Watch Kaikoura
☏ 03/319 6767 or 0800/655 121, ⓦ www.whalewatch
.co.nz. Excellent whale-watching tours ($125), featuring cultural insights by the Maori owners and an on-board DVD, showing what goes on underwater. Be warned that rough weather often cancels scheduled trips.

Annual events and festivals

Below, we've picked out the best of the annual Maori and Pacific Island events and festivals held in Aotearoa. Local tourist offices can tell you more about these, and about the many other events celebrated across the country.

January
New Year's Day: Ngati Porou celebrations (Tairawhiti), including the annual Dawn Ceremony on Mount Hikurangi. Also Whaleboat Racing Regatta at Kawhia (Tainui); and Pawarenga Sports Day on Shelly Beach at Whangape Harbour (Tai Tokerau), including beach horse racing.

Inter-Marae Sports Day (early Jan): Organised by Ngati Porou (Tairawhiti), location changes annually.

Opera in the Pa (4th Sat): Maori and Polynesian voices sing Verdi, Puccini and Mozart in Rotorua (Arawa) against a backdrop of geysers at the Maori Arts and Crafts Institute's *marae*.

February
Waitangi Day (Feb 6): A national holiday, with festivities throughout the country but notably at Waitangi, Bay of Islands (Tai Tokerau), where there's a full flotilla of *waka*, plus sports and entertainment. Also at Okains Bay (Te Waipounamu) where two *waka* are paddled, one dating from 1867.

Kapa Haka (late Feb): Biennial performance competition (odd years) pitting *waiata*, *haka*, *powhiri* and craft groups against each other.

95

March

Te Houtaewa Challenge: Annual long-distance running event at Ninety Mile Beach (Tai Tokerau), typically followed by an arts and crafts festival and a surf canoeing competition.

Wellington Dragon Boat Festival (1st weekend): Boat races, entertainment and ethnic performances in the capital, Wellington (Te Upoko o Te Ika).

Ngaruawahia Maori Regatta (March 18, 2006): Parade of traditional *waka taua* (war canoes) at Ngaruawahia (Tainui), plus *waka* racing and *waka* hurdling.

Pasifika Festival (2nd weekend): A celebration of Polynesian and Pacific Island music, culture, food and crafts drawing upwards of 150,000 people.

Polyfest (3rd weekend): Maori and Pacific Island dance and *haka* competition between secondary school groups in Auckland (Tamaki Makaurau).

May

Koroneihana Maori: Anniversary of the Maori Queen's Coronation at the Turangawaewae Marae in Ngaruawahia (Tainui).

June

Matariki, Maori New Year: Marking the time when the Pleiades constellation (known as Mata Ariki – the eyes of God) rise in the same spot as the sun – typically the time for planting new crops. Celebrations traditionally began with the sighting of the next new moon – June 27, 2006 and June 16, 2007 – but now run throughout June. Cultural events held throughout the country, particularly in Hastings (Takitimu; Ⓦ www.matarikifestival.co.nz) and at Te Papa in Wellington (Te Upoko o Te Ika). For more information see Ⓦ www.matariki .net.nz and Ⓦ www.taitokerau .co.nz/matariki.htm.

September

Tuwharetoa Festival (early Sept): Celebrating Maori culture and language through dance and performance arts in Taupo (Arawa).

November

Maori Sports Awards (late Nov): Black-tie affair where Maori sporting stars are given their due. The event is usually televised.